Choosing Heaven

Copyright © 2022 Diane Gerard.

All rights reserved.

No part of this book may be used or reproduced by any means, graphic, electronic, or mechanical, including photocopying, recording, taping or by any information storage retrieval system without the written permission of the publisher.

I.H.S. Publishers
1985 Bluestone Dr. Suite 101
St. Charles, MO 63303

636-447-6000
stationsofhope@gmail.com

Regarding the Imprimatur: According to the new Code of Canon Law issued in 1983, Canon 827, paragraphs 2 and 3, books of general religious nature no longer require an Imprimatur.

Scripture texts in this work are taken from the *New American Bible, revised edition* © 2010, 1991, 1986, 1970 Confraternity of Christian Doctrine, Washington, D.C. and are used by permission of the copyright owner. All Rights Reserved. No part of the New American Bible may be reproduced in any form without permission in writing from the copyright owner. Emphasis added throughout. Permission to use the the text of the New American Bible does not indicate review and approval of the book's content.

Cover Art: Sister Mary Beth Kemper
Graphic Design: Trese Gloriod

Printed in the United States of America

2 3 4 5 6 7 8 9 10

ISBN: 979-8-9851141-0-2

May you hear the voice of God always! —Diane

Choosing HEAVEN

Diane Gerard

I.H.S. Publishers, Saint Louis, Missouri

This book is dedicated to:

All souls in most need of God's mercy…

…and that is all of us.

Unworthy to receive God's unconditional love –
I felt the power of His love
burning so brightly that I dared not draw near –
but I knew God wanted me to draw near.

When I did draw near, I received a special message at
Eucharistic Adoration and so many subsequent blessings.

From my journal – March 23, 2020

But Thou, O Lord, remove not Thy help at a distance from me;
look towards my defense.

O my Jesus, through the merits of Thy desolate death,
deprive me not of Thy help in that *great struggle
which, in the hour of my death, I must maintain with hell.*

St. Alphonsus de Liguori

Table of Contents

Foreword x

Preface 1

Introduction 7

Part I: The Witness 13

Chapter One: The Battle for a Soul on the Brink 14

Chapter Two: Awe and Wonder! 21

Chapter Three: Reflections 23

Part II: The Choice 35

Chapter Four: Why Would Anyone Choose Hell? 36

Chapter Five: Why Choose Heaven? 120

Chapter Six: Who is Jesus? 142

Chapter Seven: The Stations of Hope 178

Chapter Eight: How Do We Choose Heaven? 212

Part III: The Chaplet 243

Chapter Nine: A Chaplet for the Love of Souls 244

Appendix: Prayers for the Chaplet 256

Acknowledgments 258

About the Author 259

Foreword

*"The kingdom of God is at hand.
Repent, and believe in the gospel."*

(Mark 1:15)

We spend our whole lives struggling to trust this proclamation of the Gospel. What does it mean for the kingdom of God to be "at hand," so near that we can almost touch it, so near that we must believe it, so near that it seems sometimes to overwhelm us, to consume us? Yet it is not fully in our grasp; when we try to grasp the truth of the Gospel we may end up clinging only to our own will. But we must continue to try. This is the spiritual life.

We are grateful to all the sinners become saints who have risked enough to share their witness of faith. While it is really impossible to express the full meaning of the kingdom come in our lifetimes, our hearts long to know it. God has called some of his disciples, through the ages, to attempt to articulate in words what is beyond words. These words can be an encouragement to all of us to continue striving, to remain trusting, to hope for eternal life now.

I have found that different saints show up in my path, sometimes unbidden. One year I had forgotten the birth name of St. Teresa Benedicta of the Cross, and as I searched it out, found myself reading the life story of Edith Stein. Through her deep devotion to the Holy Cross, I was invited to reflect more deeply on St. John of the Cross as well, which led to a deeper appreciation of the Carmelites, including Teresa of Avila and The Little Flower. So, from one absent minded search for a name I walked a month's long journey of deepening faith, like walking in a garden with my Carmelite friends.

While the saints are beautiful gifts who pray for us and walk with us, it is important to trust their own common human experience. Inevitably the saints have found their way to the heart of Christ by joining hands with fellow travelers. God sends courageous and faithful people to greet us every day and calls witnesses to risk the expression of the inexpressible so that we can be strengthened in our own response to the Gospel message.

You are, in this moment, in possession of one such precious gift. Diane Gerard has experienced a profound encounter with the Lord; God has shown Himself to her in a powerful way. She is now sharing her experience with us, that we might become more confident in our own faith, more awake to God's grace in our lives. More than anything else, Diane has come to trust God's love for us and God's desire for our salvation. It is this deep desire in the very heart of God which has compelled Diane to share her journey. Let it inspire you to connect with God's own spirit dwelling in you and to say, with Mary, "Yes" to heaven now.

Fr. Mitch Doyen, Pastor
St. John the Baptist Catholic Church
St. Louis, Missouri
September 17, 2021

Preface

He walks alone. It is a strange place, unlike any other he has been in before. He cannot even remember where he was just before this. He was strangely unaware that this was even so, until his attention shifted, and he noticed it. He had been focused on the strangeness of the place, the mist everywhere, gray mist, wafting in and out, sometimes blacker and sometimes grayer. And yet here he finds himself, walking.

As he ventures on, he hears voices. They are like voices of children, laughing, laughing at him. He cannot see the children. They seem to be there, behind the gray, always behind just enough darkness. They make him angry, he wants them to show themselves so that he can lash out at them. They will not; he yells at them anyway. Their gibes and jeers give no hint they have heard him. It frustrates him all the more.

A memory from long ago resurfaces. It carries the same impulsive anger, clutching at him from days he knew at school, as he was laughed at by other kids then. If possible, it seems the anger is even more intense than it was then, even palpable, like a film all around him.

He quickens his pace, trying to clear his head. Then, there are more voices, not children this time, but women, young women, soft and pleasant. He cannot make out what they are saying exactly, but he somehow understands what they want. They are inviting, enticing him to come after them. He realizes that he has now even begun to smile. His anger has faded entirely. The sharp contrast in his feelings draws him back to a memory from long ago. It was the first time he had tried to kiss a girl, and the exciting, gripping feeling it had given him. Ever since, he had been trying for heavier, more intense feelings of that kind. It was part of the reason he had always chased women during his life.

He peers deeply into the gray and black, hoping to catch a glimpse of the women who belong to these voices. Silhouettes are all he can manage to see. As he thinks more about these women, becomes more aroused, he begins to walk toward them a little, to where they are, off to his left. They start walking too, away from him, but still coaxing him to follow. He walks a little faster and can begin to see them ever so slightly. The haze seems to dissipate at times along the way, but there is something odd about it. The times it seems the clearest seems to coincide, not with the times he gets the closest, but with the times his desire seems the strongest.

This startles him. In this strange place, his thoughts, and even more his feelings, have a direct effect on what he sees. For some reason, fear begins to set in. He pulls back and directs his walk back to his right.

Where is he? How can he not remember how he got here? Is this only a dream? How is it that the reality he now lives in is altered by his own thinking?

He wants this to end. He wants to go back to where he was before this. He can remember some of that time now. Life was comfortable. He had decent money, a car he liked showing off, and while he had been divorced twice, was living with a woman whom he liked. Life was good. Now this. Where is he going? Where will this end?

He decides to quiet himself. His mind had been racing. Now, he just slows it all down. His walk is not fast, but not slow either. It is balanced and steady. Then, he perceives a light off in the distance, a small circle of light gradually making its way through the darkness. This light comes with feelings too. He senses they are not feelings that he generates. They come with the light. There is peace in these feelings. Somehow too, he is taken with the idea that there is knowledge in the light, an awareness that penetrates the universe. It is almost too much to handle, even at a great distance, even for only moments at a time. Then, he comes to a realization. While there is peace that came from outside him with this new experience, he first had to become peaceful to let it come. It is as if it is in the light, waiting for him.

He wonders if this peace could have been waiting for him before now, perhaps for a long time. He thinks of all the times in his life when he never let himself slow down, never let his mind be quiet. He was always pushing for something, always wanting new things, always using other people to get what he wanted.

He looks again at the light. The knowledge that is there seems to penetrate him. He is shocked and dismayed. He begins to see the times when his actions have affected others in negative ways. He sees their reactions, sees their thoughts that had been hidden from him before. He sees their self-doubts, their domino-like animosity toward others and their feeling, worst of all, a lack of love from him. He can feel the hurt, physically. It is so real. All this from when he used others as served his own purposes. It literally terrorizes him. It screams at him. He desperately wants it to stop. He yells at it to stop.

Then he also begins to see times when he extended some kindness toward others, in ways large and small. He again sees the ripple effects, in ways large and small, of these actions on still others. And again, he can feel these effects physically. This time, however, it is comforting and warm.

The more he walks toward the light, the more all of this continues, covering more and more different times in his life. He struggles with the power this is having on him, the joys and sorrows, the highs and the lows from being confronted with the effects of his actions.

Now too, he realizes something else. There is a growing divide here in this strange place of mist and haze. On one side, there is anger, sensuality, hot emotions, and the promise of pleasure. In the other direction, there is peace, peace even at the same time as there is pain with knowledge. He knows, somehow, it is one or the other for him at the end of his walk. There cannot be both. He must choose.

As all of this is running around in his head, he is getting closer to the light. It is still far off, but closer. A new sensation starts to grow. There is not just peace and self-knowledge with the light. There is something bigger, something powerful. It makes him feel attracted to the light. It makes him feel wanted. He feels as if he is wanted, more than he could have ever come close to imagining he could be wanted. It is love, tremendous love.

This strikes him as so ironic, so unfair. He rebels against this very idea. Why must he walk through this gauntlet of pain in order to find love? Then, just then, the voices return. He hears voices of people shouting at him, trying to make him angry, trying to put up a flood of anger against the peace. He also hears the sensual voices of the young women. They are entreating him all the more urgently. They, too, try to wall him off from the peace.

The smoke, the gray, the wafting fields of black, they are starting to circle him now. He continues on. The circling gets faster. Based on what he reasoned before, he knows the cloudy mists are coming from his own mind. He tries to quiet his thoughts so that the circling can slow down and allow him to see the light. He is frustrated with himself for getting in his own way. The frustration adds to his disquiet. He cannot make the mist and haze part. He tries to walk faster, as if he were to walk fast enough he could get through it, but it stays right there with him.

Then, behind him, in the trailing and circling smokiness, he senses someone is with him. He comes up alongside and then moves up ahead. He is like the others he has heard here, merely a silhouette that cannot be seen clearly. He announces, as he passes, that there need be no tough choice. He tells him that the need to feel pain for one's past, in order to get where you want to go, is a lie. He chuckles and says his way is very easy. In fact, it is downhill.

There is something disconcerting about this person. Why does he, like the other silhouetted figures, refuse to show himself. Yet what he said sounds fair. How can it be that he has to undergo pain to get to love? Why does that have to be? There were other times when staying in a relationship, whether it was a wife or member of his family, would have meant having to say he was sorry or make some other sacrifice. He had not done it those times and had made out all right. Why did it need to be any different here?

Now, he notices that the surface he had been walking on, if it could be called that, because it did not seem like any kind of a real, solid substance, has begun to decline. He feels like he is beginning to fall.

Feelings of fear start to take hold of him. He wonders where the light is. He is not sure if he is travelling toward it anymore. In the smoke and haze he could have veered off the path that led to it. He could now actually be moving away from it.

There is something about the light that will not stop pulling at him, something deep inside that will not let go. He thinks that, if there is love there, there has to be someone there who is the source of that love, someone who loves him in the unimaginable way he only so briefly felt. He grasps that he will need to take a very long journey to reach the light; he now understands that he will need to face up to each moment of his life in which he has hurt someone in even the very slightest way. Though this will take an extremely long time, he wants to find that love that he senses will be there at the end. It was so indescribable, even though he was aware of it for the briefest of moments, that he cannot dare to think of being without it. And he feels, very strongly, that what he does now will determine whether he will be with or without it, forever.

Then, he remembers how he saw the light the first time. He needs to be peaceful to let the peace in. He feverishly hopes that if he can, he can once more see the light and his way toward it.

****

Consider, the person in this story above is at that moment of death we have all heard about, have all wondered about. For each of us, that moment awaits. For each of us too, there is the question of what it will be like for us, what are the things we will see, and what, if anything, we can do now to help us through it.

While the story of the man above, told from his point of view, is a fiction, the thematic elements of it are real enough. If you are interested in how this relates to you and your life, read on. This book was written for you.

Introduction

The writing of this book came from another story, a true story over the battle for one soul that has led me into a battle for *ALL* souls. It is a Heavenly personal battle of the love of Jesus and our Blessed Mother Mary who will never, never give up on us, and of the agony and passion with which they fight right now for every soul, for my soul, for *your* soul.

The beginning of this story took place during Eucharistic Adoration – Eucharistic Adoration is prayer in the presence of the Sacred Host that has been transfigured, or changed, into the true body and blood of Jesus by the blessing of a priest. The story began at St. James Church, during a particular Eucharistic Adoration, while I was with Jesus present in the Host. The journey since is a most beautiful, painful, passionate, love-beyond-all-measure blessing meant for you, your loved ones – all of us.

I am overwhelmed and humbled to be able to share such a wonderful and powerful gift. It is not something I ever envisioned would happen to a little girl from Cheektowaga, New York. Yet, throughout my life there have been times when I have felt a complete and profound connection to God's love. I am sure you have heard of God's love before, and perhaps felt it too. This is just another story of that love, God's love for all of us.

I take comfort in Jesus' words:

> Do not worry about how you are to speak or what you are to say. You will be given at that moment what you are to say. (Matthew 10:19)

My relationship with Jesus started when I was a young girl, as early as age 4 or 5. When I was sad or frightened or troubled, I would sit on the bed in my room and listen to the Christmas song, ***Away in the Manger***. The words of the last verse of the song became a prayer for me. I prayed, in song, those words over and over. I prayed directly to Our Lord. I felt that he had come to me; I felt His presence and abiding love. I knew in my heart that He had come to me as a friend and protector, and I still feel his love in my life. To this day, whenever I even hear the song, I begin to cry.

> *Be near me, Lord Jesus. I ask thee to stay,*
> *Close by me forever, and love me, I pray.*
> *Bless all the dear children in thy tender care,*
> *And take us to Heaven to live with thee there.*

In those times, I felt completely overtaken by a feeling of a most pure love. Like the man in the preceding fictional story, it was a love so immense that it was beyond description or knowledge or ability to bear it without the support of Our Lord. I hope this story will show you that he loves you, and each of us, with just as much intensity and passion.

> God, you have taught me from my youth;
> to this day I proclaim your wonderous deeds.
> (Psalm 71:17)

The words of the song foreshadowed what I learned some 50 years later on a religious pilgrimage in 2012. What I did not understand when I was young, and would not see for another five decades, was that this little verse can be likened to a child's version of the Fatima prayer, which appears at the end of this Introduction.

I did not journey to the blessed event that occurred at Eucharistic Adoration readily or easily. My husband, Ray, is the one who wanted to go on this pilgrimage and urged me to join him. I was apprehensive. More than that, I was reluctant, even afraid, at some level, to go. Eventually, Ray simply said, "That's OK, you don't have to go, I will just go without you" – so naturally, and with the good humor that came from his taunt, I decided to go.

I told my husband that I did not understand why I did not want to go, but the truth was that I was afraid. I was afraid of letting go of myself and opening my head, heart and soul to Our Lord.

I knew in my heart, that over the years, during those times when I would get closer to Jesus, I felt overwhelmed by the love that I felt. The word "overwhelmed" is a pitifully feeble description of the love I felt from Our Lord. I understand it sounds strange, and even contradictory, to be afraid of love, but that was how I felt at the time. How can a love be so pure? So, timeless? How dare I believe I am worthy of such love?

My journey after the event was, in some ways, even more difficult. The need to write this account was urgent and compelling. I continuously thought about writing this account, spoke to many people about writing it, and even confessed to a priest my feelings of guilt for not having written it already. I was stalling what I felt compelled to do; I kept putting it off.

I spoke to a nun about my struggles with telling this story. I told her I was afraid of opening myself to Jesus – afraid of the power of His overwhelming love. She told me that the feeling of fear was the evil one's way of whispering in my ear. I had to let go of that fear and put this to words.

During these years, I have also experienced medical issues that have made the writing of this book even more challenging.

It has been a struggle. It has taken me more than nine years to overcome the obstacles and put my story to paper. As I wrote this, I continually prayed to Our Lord and Our Lady to help me to convey to you only what was in accord with God's will.

The story that follows is a true accounting of an event that happened to me at Eucharistic Adoration on March 22, 2012 and the journey that has followed.

This book is in three parts.

Part I – The Witness recounts the event that happened to me at Eucharistic Adoration at St. James. There, I was blessed to be witness to a soul at the moment of death, making the choice between Heaven and Hell. This event is meant to show us all that the choice of eternal rest in Heaven or eternal damnation in Hell is ours, by virtue of the free will granted to us by God. At the same time, we are meant to understand that Jesus and His Mother, Mary, fight for our souls. They fight so very hard for our souls because it is a fight for life for all time.

Part II – The Choice focuses on why and how the decisions and paths we take in our lives affect us in our ultimate choice of Heaven or Hell. Using familiar stories and passages from the Bible, as aided by reflections from the event at Eucharistic Adoration, these chapters provide insight into the messages God has given us for the journey to our salvation.

Additionally, in this section, there is an extended reflection on the parallels between the sufferings that Jesus endured during His life and the sufferings many of us endure today. This chapter brings clarity to the fact that Jesus empathizes with our pain in a deep and personal way, and that He is ready to forgive us for our sins.

Part III – The Chaplet describes a new way of sending our prayers to the Lord. It is called the Chaplet for the Love of Souls. Based primarily on what is known as the "Fatima Prayer," it is a plea directly to Jesus, it gives us a simple, yet powerful tool for intercessory prayer, especially when prayed in a group. Utilizing a set of rosary beads, it does not replace the blessed Rosary we have recited all our lives, it is just another way to express our love of God and one another.

In taking this journey, there are three things that I have come to more deeply understand and believe with my whole mind and soul:

1. *Prayer is the most powerful weapon in all of our struggles.*
2. *We must have the courage to pray to Jesus directly.*
3. *We must pray for EVERY soul.*

We all need prayers as much as we need to pray for one another. I pray for you, dear reader, that you may take these messages to heart and help heal the world, and *ALL* souls.

Let us pray, together, the Fatima Prayer:

> ***Oh, my Jesus.***
> ***Forgive us our sins.***
> ***Save us from the fires of Hell.***
> ***Lead all souls to Heaven,***
> ***Especially those in most need of thy mercy.***
>
> ***Amen***

Part I
The Witness

CHAPTER ONE
The Battle for a Soul on the Brink

My husband and I, and many members of our pilgrimage, were at Eucharistic Adoration at St. James Church. It was the last night of our pilgrimage.

The entire church was packed; every pew and all the aisles were filled with people sitting, kneeling and standing in every inch of space, just to be in the sacred presence of Jesus. It is almost impossible to describe how many people were in St. James.

We were standing at the back of the church in the center aisle, at the very last pew. From where I stood, I had a direct view of the monstrance that held the Sacred Host. I also had a clear view of a statue of the Blessed Mother, which was off to the right of the altar, and of the small Crucifix that was on the altar, between the monstrance and the statue.

I had two rosaries with me. The first rosary was my Father's, from his First Communion. My Grandmother had given it to me years before, and I had brought it on the pilgrimage with the intention of praying for him and his health and giving it back to him upon our return. The second rosary I bought the first day of our trip. I had been holding these two rosaries and praying on them at every event and for every blessing we received the entire week.

A light shined on the monstrance and the Sacred Host. During Eucharistic Adoration, songs were sung, and prayers were said in the multiple languages of the pilgrims. They were simple and familiar prayers and songs so all the people could participate.

But almost immediately, for me, the crowd seemed to fall away. The Sacred Host began to glow and grow larger in my sight; even the monstrance which held the Host fell away from my view. I had the need to pray directly to our Lord, Jesus with all my heart.

I began to say a prayer I remember having heard only a few times before:

> **Oh, my Jesus.**
> **Forgive us our sins.**
> **Save us from the fires of Hell.**
> **Lead all souls to Heaven,**
> **Especially those in most need of thy mercy.**
>
> **Amen**

At the time, I did not really even know the words to the prayer. I had no idea that this prayer was called the Fatima prayer, named so because it was given by our Blessed Mother to the visionaries at Fatima close to 100 years ago. I did not know the journey or all the blessings that would follow from this moment. All I knew was that the prayer was in my mind and that I desperately needed to pray that prayer with my very soul.

I first started praying the prayer on my rosary – every bead – with all my heart, in my heart and in my head. My eyes on the Host, only the Host, only on our Lord. Faster and faster, more urgency, more emphasis. I cannot remember ever being so deep in prayer. Every bead faster, the same prayer, but more powerful with every thought, every breath. Focused only on the Christ, present in the Eucharist – critically important. If the sounds of the others' prayers or a song came to me, I pushed them away. Only my prayer, only my Lord.

I felt that Blessed Mother was with me, that she was guiding me gently. If my eyes wandered over to the statue of the Blessed Mother, she urged me back to her Son – she was saying to me, "This is only a statue – look to the true Christ." It was the same message regarding with the Crucifix. Look only to the Christ – the Host – the living presence of God. Not even the golden monstrance in my view. Just the Eucharist – pure white, pure Jesus – glowing and large in my view. Mother Mary urging me directly to her Son. Tears were streaming down my face. Pain was running up and down my back.

The Host grew in my view until it filled what is the space above the altar. Only the Host, only Jesus. I no longer saw the people, the church, the statues; I did not see anything but Jesus alive in the Host.

When I finished the prayers on the beads of my rosary, I started praying the same prayer on the beads of my Father's rosary. I do not know how many times I said the prayer. Hundreds and hundreds of times. Faster still, more urgent, deeper, desperate. Praying directly to our Lord.

Suddenly, I became aware that my prayer had changed. No longer was I praying the Fatima prayer, but I was now 'speaking' directly to a soul – begging that soul to choose Heaven, to choose Jesus. In my mind I was saying, *"No, look one more time at Jesus' eyes. See his endless love. See his endless mercy. Don't choose Hell! Look again! Look one more time! Look again, look at Jesus! Don't choose Hell! Look again!"*

I was witness to a pivotal moment, a moment of death, and praying for a tortured soul standing on the brink – making the choice between Heaven and Hell. I do not know whose soul – it did not matter. I did not "see" the soul or Jesus, other than the Host, but just "knew" with all my being that the battle for this soul was being waged. Jesus and Mary against the evil one. The soul had turned away from Heaven and was moving toward Hell. I felt the agony of Jesus and Mary as they saw the soul turn away and as they knew the decision of the soul was made out of free will.

The same words over and over in my head, endless tears, agony for that desperate soul. *"Don't choose Hell! Look at His eyes! See His endless mercy, His endless love. Don't look away! Don't choose Hell! Don't choose Hell!"* I screamed in my mind.

At some point, I became aware that I was speaking directly to Jesus – my eyes still fixed on the Body of Christ in the Host and begging him to save this tortured soul. ***"Dear Jesus, look again, one more time. Look into his eyes, don't let him choose Hell. Look again! Please, please Dear Jesus!!"***

At the same time, begging, pleading to the troubled soul, "Look again. Look at His eyes, His endless love, His endless mercy. ***Don't choose Hell! Don't choose Hell! Don't choose Hell!"***

Faster, deeper, pleading. Tears. Terrible agony and pain shooting up my back. The pain was hot and like a knife. Searing. Never before had I felt such pain, but my eyes were still fixed on our Lord in the Eucharist, shining, brighter, bigger, stronger.

A war for a soul. Any soul, this soul. A 'knowing' then came to me, that our Blessed Lord Jesus and our Blessed Mother were fighting a tremendous battle to save this soul, and that they fight this hard to save *every* soul! The fight is *this* hard, *every* time, because it is a fight for eternal salvation!

Then I was begging Jesus, ***"No! Jesus you MUST save this soul! You MUST save ten souls, a hundred souls, a million souls, a billion souls!"*** over and over. It was a plea that was pure and from the heart. ***"Jesus you must save this soul! You must save ten souls, a hundred souls, a million souls, a billion souls! Please, dear Jesus!"***

Following the event, I could hardly believe I would have the audacity to speak to our Lord this way, but at the time, it was the prayer that needed to be prayed and Jesus was with me, guiding me. It took a long time, and much reflection afterwards, to understand that I was joining my prayer for souls to that of Jesus and our Blessed Mother and raising those prayers to God.

I am not sure how long it all lasted – the tears, the pain, the agony over the soul – so much to bear. Then I realized I was back to the original prayer.

Oh, my Jesus.
Forgive us our sins.
Save us from the fires of Hell.
Lead all souls to Heaven,
Especially those in most need of thy mercy.

Amen

At some point, a seat opened, and our friend, Bob, tried to lead me to the seat. At first, I resisted, I pulled away, I did not want anything to break the connection with our Lord. But then he led me to a spot. I kneeled and continued my prayer. The pain in my back was still there, still agonizing, paralyzing, red hot. I understood, however, that the pain, was nothing compared to losing the soul to Hell. I had an overwhelming sense of urgency to not let this soul go. Pleading, begging our Lord. The tears came harder, faster.

Then, I felt a warm 'hug' start at my back and embrace my entire body. It was as soft as angel wings and comforting. Instantly, the pain in my back vanished.

Then, it was the end. The next thing I remember was my husband, Ray, telling me that we had to leave. We were the last people in the church. The lights were going off.

They had taken my Lord away, yet I have no recollection of them taking the Host or the monstrance away. The people were gone, I do not remember people moving or leaving or any sounds. It seems impossible since there were so many people in the church.

I was sobbing. Spent. Empty. I only remember my husband helping me up, we had to go.

I did not think my legs could even carry me out of the church. Ray helped me out the door. We got out of the church and I managed to walk just a few steps and sat on the steps of the church.

I told my husband, "I can't do this. I'm not strong enough. It's too hard!" The reality of the moment carried a feeling of so much burden, yet so much love! He told me, "Pray."

We walked across the street to meet up with our friends in a restaurant. I did not know how, or if, I would be able to join the comradery; it felt like such frivolity all of a sudden. I simply wanted to contemplate the moment in silent contemplation and prayer.

The members of our group were there already. We took seats near the windows, near Bob and Arlyss. I looked a mess from crying. I tried to explain to them what had happened at church, but it was noisy, and they could not really hear the details. I was still shaking from the event and was not sure what to do next, what to think. I could only believe.

I started replaying the event in my mind. There was a swirl of thoughts and emotions. I did not know where to begin.

After the event, I did not know the answer to what had happened to that tortured soul. I did not know if ultimately the soul had chosen Heaven or Hell. I had no sense of time related to the soul, either. I did not know if this was happening in that moment or a thousand years in the past or a thousand years in the future. It felt timeless.

I realized that the warm 'hug' that took away the searing pain down my back could not have been from a person, as it would have been impossible, given where and how I was kneeling, and so it was a special blessing sent from our Lord. All I know is that, with the "hug," the pain in my back was gone in an instant, as quickly as it had come.

What I had witnessed was real. It was the most real experience of my life. I was immersed in the experience. It would be easier for me to deny that the sun rises in the morning than to deny this experience.

Part of what confirms for me that this was all real, is that I feel no desire, surprisingly to myself, to know who the soul was or what happened to him or her. I am at peace that I am not supposed to know.

I have come to believe that the message of the witness is about choices and saving souls. The message is about free will, and about how our own choices lead us on a path to eternal rest with God, or eternal damnation with the devil.

Additionally, what I do know, and what we are all supposed to understand, is the intensity of the battle over ***EVERY*** soul, ***EVERY*** time. ***YOUR*** soul. ***MY*** soul. Jesus and Blessed Mother fight this fight for ***EVERY*** soul, every time! We are not in this fight alone.

Prayer and the rosary are our most powerful weapons; for ourselves, for our loved ones, for everyone! We need to pray for one another. We need to pray for the souls in most need of God's mercy. We need to pray for the souls in purgatory and for the souls in this world and the next. We need to pray, pray, pray.

For, as Jesus tells us:

> ***Ask and it will be given to you; seek and you will find; knock and the door will be opened to you. For everyone who asks, receives; and the one who seeks, finds; and to the one who knocks, the door will be opened.*** (Matthew 7:7-8)

CHAPTER TWO
Awe and Wonder!

I was in awe! What wonder! After the experience at St. James, all I could think was, ***"It's All True!"*** Everything. Everything I had learned in my life and believed was true!

There really is a Heaven! There really is a Hell. There is a God that loves us! There is an evil one who wants our souls! Jesus and Mary are there for us and fight for our souls! I was there, I had experienced it! I knew to my very soul that it was ***ALL TRUE***!

> Jesus said: "Do not think that I have come to abolish the law or the prophets. I have come not to abolish but to fulfill. Amen, I say to you, until heaven and earth pass away, not the smallest letter or the smallest part of a letter will pass from the law, until all things have taken place." (Matthew 5:17-18)

There was so much joy. So much love. So much mercy. So much beauty in the world that God has given us. So much wonder in the people God had placed in my garden.

I could not contain myself. I wanted to shout it from the mountain tops. I was as giddy as Ebenezer Scrooge on Christmas morning!! I did not know what to do first.

Golden Raindrops

I could feel the countless blessings that were showering around me like soft, golden raindrops. I could feel that they were warm and comforting – like a spring rain – and the blessings themselves were happy and joyous to serve God. They were so happy to be doing God's work of showering us all with blessings that when they hit the ground, they bounced and multiplied into more blessings.

Thus says the Lord:
Yet just as from the heavens
  the rain and snow come down
And do not return there
  till they have watered the earth,
  making it fertile and fruitful,
Giving seed to the one who sows
  and bread to the one who eats,
So shall my word be
  that goes forth from my mouth;
It shall not return to me empty,
  but shall do what pleases me,
  achieving the end for which I sent it.
(Isaiah 55:10-11)

I tried to put the messages I received into action but stumbled along the way. At the same time, I was trying to comprehend what had occurred at St. James and what was its meaning.

I know it is a lot to take in, and you may be skeptical, dear reader. So, just think, for a moment, about a person that you love with all your heart – a son, a daughter, your spouse, a friend or your grandchild. Imagine that this person is at the end of his or her life and must make the final choice between Heaven or Hell. Imagine that you can see this person turning away from Heaven and walking toward Hell. You understand that this person has the free will to choose, but you are made to watch them go. There is nothing you can do to intervene at this point. What agony would you feel? What would you think? What would you pray?

As you read this book, I invite you to think about that person, and his or her soul. Think about yourself and your own choices. And, please, pray for all souls with all your heart.

CHAPTER THREE
Reflections

So much had happened at the Eucharistic Adoration event. I was amazed, overwhelmed! I was humbled and ecstatic and confused all at the same time. I knew that the message I had received was that Our Mother and Our Lord Jesus fight for every soul, for life with God for all time. The words *"every soul"* and *"all time"* had tremendously more meaning to me than ever. I kept repeating the words, *"every"* and *"all,"* as if they were treasures of incalculable value that I had been given. I did not know what to think, all I could do was feel.

I kept repeating to myself, *"It's all true! It's all true!"* I had never had so much conviction in my beliefs about Our Father, Jesus Christ, and Our Lady, the Bible and Heaven. For just a moment, I was given the blessing of seeing beyond the veil.

My mind was racing. Where to start? What's next? What did God want me to do with all of this? I did not know where to begin. I did record it in my journal so that I would never forget the details. I was writing so fast that my hand ached.

I felt completely filled with the Holy Spirit! I could feel Blessed Mother's love near me and gently guiding me. I could not wait to share the news of what had happened to me. Over the next few weeks, as Ray and I met with our family and friends, we told them of all the things we had seen and experienced, and we told them of the battle for the tortured soul.

I told anyone I could get to listen, that Jesus and Mary fight for *every* soul, no matter what you have done. They will fight a tremendous battle for you because the battle is for your very soul. Jesus does not want to lose even one of his sheep, and Blessed Mother does not want to lose even one of her children. They fight this hard, because the evil one fights just as hard. This is a love beyond all measure, for every soul, for life for all time.

I started seeing more and more blessings in my life; I was completely aware of even the smallest of gifts. As my Grandmother would often say, "Thank God for that blessing!"

I told everyone that blessings from Heaven were falling all around us like golden raindrops. They were warm and comforting, and the raindrops were so happy, that, when they hit the ground they bounced for joy!

I felt absolutely surrounded by the joy and comfort of Our Lady and Our Lord. I cried with joy, I laughed with joy, I smiled with joy that was boundless. I felt that this is how Jesus wants us to feel his love all the time, but that earthly anxieties, too often, get in the way.

Over many months, I reflected on the trip and what it meant. I knew what happened to me at St. James church that night was real. To me, it was a miracle, a special view into the love of Jesus, and Mary, that needed to be shared with the world, but how? And, what would I say? And, why little old me? I am not a priest or nun or theologian. I have no special knowledge, just my full and complete belief that this really did happen.

Strange, but all my life, I would sing the song, "Here I am Lord" with the hope that I could someday be useful to God. I always desired to live the Gospel. But then, when this happened, it set me back and frightened me. Who was I to receive such a gift? Would I be able to find a way to bring it to life for others? I felt completely unworthy to receive the gift, and equally unworthy and unable to find a way to share it.

> Behold the Lamb of God, behold him who takes away the sins of the world. Blessed are those called to the supper of the Lamb.

> Lord, I am not worthy that you should enter under my roof, but only say the word and my soul shall be healed.
>
> (Communion Rite, Invitation to Communion, Catholic Mass)

At the Adoration event, the Lamb of God was ready to take away the sins of that tortured soul. The soul only needed to turn around and look to Jesus and repent. I understood that we are *ALL* called to the supper of the Lamb. I felt, more than ever, unworthy, but loved beyond measure. But, I felt, the message was not so much about "worthiness;" as it was about love and mercy.

The peace and love and joy I was feeling from Our Lady was so comforting. I was like a child wrapped in her mother's embrace. Like a child holding her mother's hand as I crossed the street for the first time. I could not find any words to describe the love.

I knew only a few things for sure.

1. Blessed Mother has visited the whole world, through many apparitions over the years, on behalf of her Son, for the salvation of souls, all souls, your soul.
2. Sins, whether they are big or small, come from Satan, and he is working very hard in the world even today.
3. What happened to me at St. James was real, and somehow, some way, I was meant to share it with you.

But, over the months, as I came back into the world, it became harder and harder to hold on to those feelings. I was living back in the world. Taking care of my family. Working a stressful job. Trying to find a balance between this world and the next. It became harder and harder to find the time to even contemplate what I was to do.

Over time, I started keeping my story to myself, rather than sharing it. What would others think of me if they found out my story?

Would they think I was crazy? Did I have the faith of the early Christians? Or, was I going to hide from this? I was feeling guilty and joyous at the same time. This was not meant only for me. But, where was I to take it? These feelings of doubt and confusion could not have been coming from Our Lord or Blessed Mother.

One of the things that helped me was pondering the words of St. Teresa of Avila. It is comforting to know that the saints struggle with the same things we do. St. Teresa said:

> On one hand, God was calling me. On the other, I was following the world. All the things of God made me happy; those of the world held me bound... I was not able to shut myself within myself... instead, I shut myself within a thousand vanities.

In a book about St. Teresa's life, the author recounts, "Over the next several years, God granted Teresa so many experiences of his presence in prayer that she feared she was being misled by the devil. Throughout her life, she could not understand why such wonderful things had been granted to her. She always felt radically unworthy of them." St. Teresa wrote:

> Let nothing disturb you
> Let nothing frighten you.
> All things pass away;
> God never changes.
> Patience obtains all things.
> He who has God
> Finds he lacks nothing;
> God alone suffices.

Let nothing disturb you. Let nothing disturb you. God alone suffices. What a powerful and comforting message. How could I manage to live this message in this world?

But I, like St. Teresa, felt both the call of God and the distraction of the world. It has taken me many years to put the world aside enough to write down my story. Through this time, I have felt the tug of needing to write it all the time, and the guilt of not taking the time to do it. Still, I thank God for all the blessings in my life, including the miracle I felt at St. James and the time he has granted me to write this story. I thank Jesus for the comfort he gives:

> "Do not let your hearts be troubled. You have faith in God; have faith also in me." [Jesus said] "I am the way and the truth and the life. No one comes to the Father except through me." (John 14:1,6)

The Fatima Prayer

In 1917, at Fatima, Our Lady gave us a beautiful prayer that appeals directly to her Son. At that time, she appeared to three shepherd children. She appeared in a remote, hilly area called Cova da Iria in Portugal. The children were aged 7 to 10 years old when they received their apparitions of Our Lady.

There were six apparitions in total. On the last of her apparitions, Our Lady performed a miracle in front of a crowd of approximately 70,000 people who had gathered to see her. It is called the Miracle of the Sun, and the people saw the sun grow exceedingly large, it danced and appeared to plummet down to earth, before returning to normal. Of the 70,000 who were present, not only believers, but government officials, newspaper reporters, policemen and sceptics, all admitted afterwards that they had seen the miracle. Our Lady offered this miracle as proof of what the children had seen and been told. It was responsible for many conversions to faith.

In her messages to the children at Fatima, Our Lady called on all the world to pray the Rosary and consecrate Russia to her care, to support peace, and to prevent war. Many believe that if her messages had been followed more faithfully, World War II may not have happened.

During the third apparition to Francisco, Lucia and Jacinta, Blessed Mother gave us a simple and beautiful prayer to her son. Our Lady told them:

> *"When you pray the Rosary, say after each mystery, 'O my Jesus, pardon us and deliver us from the fire of Hell. Draw all souls to Heaven, especially those in most need.'"*

It is a simple and powerful little prayer that has been added to the Rosary prayers. But somehow, I had missed this in my Catholic upbringing. I had heard this little prayer a few times before my pilgrimage, but it was not a regular part of reciting the Rosary for me. On the pilgrimage, our group said it when we prayed the Rosary. But during those times, I just listened because I did not think I knew the words.

During that glorious battle for a soul at St. James, and ever since, it is a prayer that is often in my mind and heart, and on my lips. No matter what tragic or terrible thing I see on the news, or trouble I hear from family or friends, this prayer comes immediately to mind. It is healing for me to say it. I feel the need to help Jesus save all souls, not just the souls who are harmed by the violence or struggles of the world, but for those souls who have caused the pain.

> *Oh, my Jesus.*
> *Forgive us our sins.*
> *Save us from the fires of Hell.*
> *Lead all souls to Heaven,*
> *Especially those in most need of thy mercy.*
>
> *Amen*

Our Lady wants all her children to be saved. One of Our Lady's key messages through all her apparitions over time is repentance and reconciliation. She stresses that we must be honest and contrite in our prayers to Our Lord Jesus. Through reconciliation, she wants us not only to confess our sins, but to choose a better path going forward. No sin is too great for Our Lord to forgive if we approach Him with a humble and contrite heart.

We must approach Jesus with faith and an honest reflection of our own lives. We must be like the centurion, in Matthew's Gospel, who fully understands his own sins but still humbly seeks healing, for his servant, from Jesus.

> "Lord, I am not worthy to have you enter under my roof; only say the word and my servant will be healed." Jesus said to the centurion, "You may go; as you have believed, let it be done for you." And at that very hour [his] servant was healed. (Matthew 8:8,13)

What Did You See?

Many people have asked me, after hearing the story of the Adoration event, "What did you see?" Was it a "vision"? The simple answer is that I "saw" nothing more than what I have described, however, the experience was much more than simply visual.

I "saw" the Eucharist grow large in my view. The Eucharist, the Host, alone, without the monstrance that held it on the altar, filled the space above the altar. As a Catholic, I believe that, at Mass, the host is transformed into the actual presence of Jesus by the priest. During the event, I did not see the personage of Jesus, other than the very large Sacred Host, which of course, is Jesus.

It has occurred to me, as I have pondered the event since then, that the vision of the Eucharist growing large over the altar in the church parallels, in some ways, the Miracle of the Sun in Fatima. While the sun grew large and intense for the witnesses at Fatima, the light for all the world to see, the Eucharist grew large for me at St. James. Since the Eucharist *is* the Son of God, amazingly, as I was praying the Fatima Prayer, I was seeing ***the Son***.

I did not have a "vision" of anything else. I did not "see" the lost soul or Blessed Mother. At the deepest parts of the event, I did not see the monstrance, or the church, or the people around me. I did not hear the music or any other sounds. I was not aware of anything except what I was experiencing.

I do not know how else to explain it, but the pain that I felt shooting down my back was more "real" and powerful than any pain I have ever experienced in the reality of my life. It was like someone had taken a sword that had been in the hottest fire and stuck it down my entire spine. Imagine a bolt of lightning in heat and intensity, but constant, unmoving. Somehow, I knew, that the pain was meant to be a mere reflection of Christ's agony over the potential choice of that soul.

During the event I had a sense of being completely immersed in what was happening. It was a sense, that there was no space between me and what was happening, I was "within" it. I was part of it, but my presence had no effect on what was happening. I wanted desperately to help this soul. I do not know if my petitions and screams reached the soul, but I knew it was his or her free will choice to make.

I had no sense of time either. I had the sensation that time was not a factor in the event, that it could have been happening at that moment, or at some other time in the past or future – there was an always and everywhere essence to it.

I felt that Blessed Mother was guiding me, deeper and deeper into the moment and toward her Son. I felt the amazingly gentle and loving presence of Jesus. It was all encompassing and overwhelming beyond measure. I did not "see" his eyes of love, but I felt them with my whole being.

I did not "see" the tortured soul, but I "knew" that he or she was standing on the brink of the choice between Heaven and Hell. The soul was turning away from Heaven and Jesus' love. But Jesus and Blessed Mother were right there fighting for him or her. The soul had free will. But Jesus and Mary were fighting with all their might and love to save this soul, to not watch the soul choose Hell because it is a choice for separation from God's love for all time. I wanted, with my whole being, for the soul to turn around and look at Jesus' eyes and see his love. I felt that if he or she caught one little glimpse of the intensity of Jesus' love, there would be no way for him or her to choose Hell.

I have come to understand, and wish to share with you, dear reader, that Mary and Jesus fight this hard every time, for every soul, over all time. They fight this hard for you at every moment, this moment. No matter what you think you have done, no matter how far away from Jesus and Mary you may feel right now, they are as close as your skin and your breath and your heart. They want to be with you, now and forever. They will not give up, and they will meet you wherever you are.

On Praying for All Souls

What that battle for the soul showed me, is that even at the very hour of death, Blessed Mother and Jesus are fighting for every soul, no matter how far away they seem. They do not want to lose *any* soul, because the fight is for *every* soul. They will be there to meet each of us at the hour of death, fighting for us to choose Heaven and not Hell. However, ultimately, it is our conscious free will choice.

I have since reflected on my own sins and failings through the lens of the messages of Our Lady, given in apparitions at Fatima, Lourdes, Guadalupe, and many stories of the Bible. I am deeply saddened that my sins have caused pain to anyone around me and have helped to nail Jesus to the cross. I hope to never choose Hell, or even come close. I pray for you, dear reader, that your soul is never even close to choosing Hell either.

Another one of the things that caused me the most reflection, over time, was my desperate cry to Jesus, during the Eucharistic

Adoration event, that He save not only that one tortured soul, but also that He save ten souls, a hundred souls, a million souls, a billion souls. I was crying, begging, screaming, demanding this over and over in my mind.

It was only afterwards that I was shocked by the audacity of my thoughts and words. Who was I to demand such a thing from Our Lord, and with such passion and conviction? I simply remember feeling at the time that Jesus was with me, and that it was the most important thing to ask. As Our Lady has told us through many visionaries, it is important for us to join our prayers with hers, and the will of her Son, to support their plans for the world.

But imagine, if you were given a special moment with Jesus, what would you ask? What would be the most important thing to ask from him? Yes, it is important to pray for someone's earthly need, to pray for relief from cancer, to pray to stop the fighting in one's family, or for a new job. However, if you could ask for only one thing for the people you love the most, would it not ultimately be for the salvation of their souls? Is it not our souls, our eternal souls, that are the greatest gifts from God? That is why Jesus came to earth for us.

I think back over the years now and see that my prayers before now have always been wishy-washy. "Whatever is your will, God," was my standard prayer. I reasoned that if I did not ask for anything specific, I was being humble, and that it meant I was surrendering my will to God. I rarely, practically never, asked for anything in particular for myself, even in times of desperate struggle, pain or need.

It was easier to ask for specific things for others, but I did not feel worthy to ask for anything specific for myself. But now I have come to understand that God wants our prayers to join with his so they can multiply and be fulfilled. That *is* the power of prayer, and that is why we need to pray our intentions on the beads of the Chaplet (see Chapter Nine).

If we ask humbly, and in line with God's will, it is bold and audacious to ask for the biggest things we need and want, for ourselves, for others, and for the world. We must remember that it is God that we are asking. He is capable of the biggest things. He wants us to ask for them.

When we do not express our needs to the Lord, it can only be because we think one of four things, none of which can be true:

1. That our sins are too great for us to be heard, or
2. That God is either not merciful enough or incapable of forgiving our sins, or
3. That our problems are too small, too petty, or unworthy of God's love, or
4. That we can handle all the sufferings, worries and dreams of the world by ourselves, without the help of God.

A reading from Isaiah brought it home for me.

> Again the LORD spoke to Ahaz: Ask for a sign from the LORD, your God; let it be deep as Sheol [the netherworld], or high as the sky! But Ahaz answered, "I will not ask! I will not tempt the LORD!" Then he said: Listen, house of David! Is it not enough that you weary human beings? Must you also weary my God? (Isaiah 7:10-13)

So, now I believe that in that moment with that tortured soul, I was meant to ask Jesus to save souls. The Lord wants us to ask for all we need, whatever we need, just as a child would ask his father. We all responsible for each other and need to pray for our brothers and sisters to be saved. We must pray for *all* souls and *all* the world.

Part II
The Choice

Chapter Four
Why Would Anyone Choose Hell?

Over the years, after I have shared the Adoration story about the soul turning away from Jesus at the moment of death, many people have asked me, "Why would anyone choose Hell?" It is the next logical question. Clearly, if a soul was standing on the brink and Jesus appeared in his full glory, and the devil was showing his true intentions and fangs, I would dare to venture that the soul would most assuredly want to go to Heaven.

But, considering my experience, I do not believe that this is how that moment of ultimate choice will present itself. It will not be quite that easy.

Let us consider: what if, at that moment, our senses are clouded by our own past actions, and we cannot see clearly who is calling to us?

What if, the evil one stands tempting us with the pleasures and deceptions that most appealed to us in our lives?

What if, following the voice of Jesus to Heaven also required a true review of, and atonement for, our earthly lives?

Often enough, we tend to stay on paths we know, ones to which we have become accustomed. If we have trained ourselves to listen to the voice of the evil one during our lives, we may very likely be unable to recognize the voice of the Lord when we need to hear it the most.

If all this is true, is there anything that we can do to prepare for that moment, that choice? Are there things we should have, or could have, known ahead of time? Where are we to look for answers?

Understanding These Questions Through the Adoration Event

My witness, at the Adoration event, to the soul standing on the brink between Heaven and Hell, made one thing very clear to me. We are not in this battle alone. Both Jesus and his blessed mother, Mary, are right there. They desire with all their hearts for *every* soul to be saved. They do not wish for even one soul to be lost.

They are in complete agony of heart when any soul rejects the Father, turns away from them, walks away from Heaven. During the Adoration event I felt that the pain I felt shooting down my back represented their agony of heart. The pain that I felt was beyond words to describe. I can only say that it was searing hot, like a burning sword that went straight down my back. It was a pain like I have never felt in my life, and yet, I stood in the middle of that aisle in church and did not move or scream or run away. It was many, many times worse than the pains of childbirth or the worst migraine I have ever felt, and my migraines can leave me rolling around on the bed in a fetal position. Somehow, I believe, the pain was meant to be a physical representation of how hard Jesus and Mary fight for every soul and how much pain they suffer when a soul turns away.

I wonder now, how, I was able to bear it, but it can only be a blessing from our Lord. The pain continued for most of the event, but since the event was timeless, I do not really know how long it lasted. It lasted until that moment in the pew when I felt what seemed like a warm hug that surrounded me. That was close to the end of the Adoration hour, based upon what my friend Bob told me was the time when he moved me into the pew. I was kneeling in the pew and that "hug" surrounded me and was meant to comfort me.

The "hug" that took the pain away was also beyond words to describe. It was soft like feathers, and warm. It enveloped my body from back to front, but it was so light, that it did not even feel like it touched me, though I know that it did.

I also have the sensation that the hug was blue, a light, but intense sky blue, yet unlike any blue I have ever seen. It is strange to think of this hug, this feeling, being a color. At the moment of the hug, instantly, the pain in my back vanished.

It is possible that this was the moment when the priests removed the Eucharist from the altar, but I cannot be sure of any specific time during the event. I do not have any recollection of the Eucharist being removed from the altar. I have no recollection of the sights and sounds of the hundreds of people leaving the church. It seems impossible, but the next moment that I remember was Ray telling me that we had to leave the church. The church was empty, and people were turning off the lights. How did all of that happen and I have no sensation or memory of it?

Again, I tell you, I have no knowledge of what eventually happened to that soul. It is not for me or you to know. If we knew, it might be too easy for us to make excuses, either way, about why that soul made it into Heaven or Hell.

I believe, instead, the Adoration event is about each of us. It is meant to help us understand that we have free will right up to the moment of our deaths. Each of us chooses Heaven or Hell, Jesus or the devil. At that moment, we will either follow our Lord and the truth, or the empty promises and temptations and lies of the evil one. That moment in our lives is the ultimate battle for our souls. The moment that is the pinnacle of our life here on earth, and the moment we transition to eternity, comes down to our choice, our free will to choose.

We can have confidence, however, that we are not in the battle alone. We must always remember that Our Lord, Jesus Christ, is right there for us. His mother is standing by his side. They fight for **your soul** and for my soul and for **every soul** because they know it is a fight against the evil one, and the outcome is for eternity.

A Healing Blessing at Mass

Why would anyone choose to walk away from Jesus and toward Hell? I prayed on this question literally for years. I prayed to understand how it could be that anyone would ever choose Hell. I began to get the answer following a "healing blessing" at Mass a few years after the Adoration event.

At some point during that Mass, our Pastor, Reverend Mitchell Doyen, called anyone in need of healing prayers up onto the altar. He had us stand in front of the altar facing the congregation. I was standing in the middle of a group of about a dozen or more people. I felt in need of prayers for healing of both body and mind as I struggled with challenges in my life brought about by some medical conditions.

The priest came to each of us individually, anointed our hands with sacred oil, and said a little prayer for healing. Next he anointed our foreheads with the sacred oil and touched our faces. As he cupped the side of my face with his hand, I felt a tingling of electricity starting at my face and running down my entire body. I was surprised but did not pull back. At that moment, I had no sense of what this might be or what it might mean. I believe that the priest also felt something at that moment, because he paused and looked directly into my eyes with a manner that suggested a sense of question or surprise that had not been on his face before.

Little did I know that, following that Mass, this book would take on an entirely new direction, and a major part of this book had yet to be written. It was the Bible, the words of Jesus himself, the inspired writings of the New Testament authors, all the writings in the Old Testament, and words from the Mass, which contained the keys to understanding my enduring question.

In the days and weeks following the healing service at Mass, I kept saying to people that this book was pouring out of me. Then I remembered the words of Psalm 23:

> You anoint my head with oil;
> my cup overflows.
> (Psalm 23)

That is what happened. My head was anointed with oil and these words have overflowed!

> Amen, amen, I say to you, no slave is greater than his master nor any messenger greater than the one who sent him. (John 13:16)

What has flowed into this book is a new compilation of the messages we have heard many times from the Bible. All the words are there, all the messages are there, and all the instructions are there. Perhaps, for some of you reading this book, they have been hiding in plain sight.

Overlooking Many Truths

Many of us, sadly even I, have stopped really hearing and understanding the messages the Lord has sent us because the words and stories may have become so familiar over time, or because they seem thousands of years distant to us. Our minds may wander at Mass as the lector proclaims a familiar passage. We may gloss over the priest's words in a homily that has a message we think we have heard before. We may wonder how an event from 2,000 or 3,000 years ago relates to our own lives.

As we hear the stories every week at Mass, or read some of them for ourselves, do we really pay attention to the power of those messages from our Father? Do we really comprehend how they are all connected to one another and to God's ultimate plan for salvation? Has anyone ever even tried to explain to us how they are connected to one another? Do we see our own lives in the stories? Do we really understand them to be the roadmap to Heaven rather than Hell?

In this book, I will try here to pull out some of those messages. I pray, that by the grace of our Father, my words will flow in a way that you may hear these messages and see them in a new light. I pray that they will touch your heart and bring you closer to our Lord.

As I stated earlier, since the Adoration event, words, single words, and sometimes a few words, have become like flashing neon signs to me. Simple words, such as "every" and "each" and "all" have an entirely new meaning for me. When Jesus tells us that God wants to save "every" soul, he means **EVERY** soul. Every - one. All of us. He does not want to lose even one of us to the evil one. What a powerful message.

To begin, the following passage from John reflects the goal of Our Father and Jesus to save *every* soul.

> Jesus said to them, "I am the bread of life; whoever comes to me will never hunger, and whoever believes in me will never thirst. But I told you that although you have seen [me], you did not believe. Everything that the Father gives me will come to me, and I will not reject ***anyone*** who comes to me, because I came down from heaven not to do my own will but the will of the one who sent me, ***And this is the will of the one who sent me, that I should not lose anything of what he gave me, but that I should raise it [on] the last day.*** For this is the will of my Father, that *everyone* who sees the Son and believes in him may have eternal life, and I shall raise him [on] the last day. (John 6:35-40)

Over the next several months and years, words and passages of the Bible became like beacons to me. The words seemed to almost glow on the page, and I began to find new and amazing connections.

I started collecting little scraps of paper with Bible quotes and snippets of prayers from the Mass. They ended up all over my house. There were so many on the kitchen table that we could hardly find a space to eat dinner. They ended up on the floor and on the table in my bedroom. I taped them in my journal. I began to see how they all were connected and purposeful.

The next chapters of this book include some of the scriptural messages and guidance we have received from God. I pray at least a few of the connections contained here will help you on your own path of self-discovery. What you find may be different. That is the way it is meant to be. Even the same words may take on a new meaning at different points in our lives.

In order to see the roadmap to Heaven, we must believe there are important messages in everything that God has shared with us, not just the New Testament, but also the Old Testament, the Psalms, the Mass and the Sacraments. It's all in there. Everything we need to know has been given to us. Everything.

> For whatever was written previously was written for our instruction, that by endurance and by the encouragement of the scriptures we might have hope. May the God of endurance and encouragement grant you to think in harmony with one another, in keeping with Christ Jesus, that with one accord you may with one voice glorify the God and Father of our Lord Jesus Christ. (Romans 15:4-6)

Growing up as a Catholic Christian, my focus had always been on the New Testament even though readings from the Old Testament and Psalms were included in the Mass and daily readings. My thoughts have been, "Of course my focus is on the New Testament, shouldn't it be? After all, I am a Christian, I follow Christ, and he has given us a 'New Covenant.' Why would I need to pay attention to the Old Testament and Psalms? They are really hard to understand anyway." But, as I began to follow the lead and guidance of the Holy Spirit, I began to comprehend that Jesus continually points us back to the messages of the Old Testament as a roadmap to our eternal life with God.

Maybe, dear reader, this is stating the obvious for you. I think to myself, who am I to be interpreting the Bible, of all things, for others? I am not a trained scholar of the Word. I have no training in biblical things. Countless others have written about God's love and mercy and guidance over the years. Who am I to even think that this will help even one soul?

The Bible is the living Word. It is God speaking to us. He gave it to us. He wants us to read it, to let it speak to us, to revive or rejuvenate our feelings for Him. Spending time with passages from the Bible can lead to so much good. It is not for me to offer interpretations of the Bible with any doctrinal authority. It is enough to spend time with the Bible and with you, to bring the passages to you with certain reflections and ask that the Holy Spirit allow you to hear, from Him, what He wills for you to hear.

I must warn you, that while this road is full of mercy and love, it is also a road paved by the Father's direction and correction. Some of this may make us feel uncomfortable in our modern day and modern ways. Many of us have fallen away from faith ourselves, and we have forgotten to pass the messages of faith onto our children. Yet, if not for ourselves, would we not want to save the souls of our children? Many of us are intimidated by others in society that think that belief in God and the Commandments is old-fashioned or irrelevant.

I am Catholic. I am proud of my beliefs and faith, and I believe that the Catholic Church was founded by Jesus himself and remains a continuing true faith. I believe that Jesus is truly present in the Eucharist we receive at Communion in Mass, and I believe he is truly present when we are with him at Adoration.

But this book is about saving souls. It is about converting you to a solid and everlasting relationship with God. It is about helping you to know that God will meet you where you are. He desires with all his heart that you come to him. Whoever you are. Whatever the circumstances.

He knows you and he knows your circumstances. He has called you by name even before you were conceived in the womb. Whatever your circumstances, it will not surprise him. He knows your desires and hurts and sins and fears and joys before you can even tell him. But the blessings from God fall from the sky like warm, gentle, golden raindrops. They fall on you and they fall on me.

Stop right now! Try to feel their warmth and comfort. Let them hug you and give you the courage and strength to move forward in your beliefs.

> Then Peter proceeded to speak and said, "In truth, I see that God shows no partiality. Rather, in every nation whoever fears him and acts uprightly is acceptable to him. You know the word [that] he sent to the Israelites as he proclaimed peace through Jesus Christ, who is Lord of all,...how God anointed Jesus of Nazareth with the holy Spirit and power. He went about doing good and healing all those oppressed by the devil, for God was with him. (Acts 10:34-36, 38)

We must hold fast to belief in God, because the lesson of the soul on the brink, the soul who was walking away from Jesus and choosing Hell means, *it's all true!*

So, as we begin, let us start with a simple, humble prayer:

> *Open our hearts, O Lord,*
>
> *to listen to the words of your Son.* (cf. Acts: 16:14)

Jesus tells us:

> "Do not let your hearts be troubled. You have faith

in God; have faith also in me. In my Father's house there are many dwelling places. If there were not, would I have told you that I am going to prepare a place for you? And if I go and prepare a place for you, I will come back again and take you to myself, so that where I am you also may be. Where [I] am going you know the way." Thomas said to him, "Master, we do not know where you are going; how can we know the way?" Jesus said to him, "I am the way and the truth and the life. No one comes to the Father except through me. If you know me, then you will also know my Father. From now on you do know him and have seen him." (John 14:1-7)

In this one passage, Jesus gives us the path to eternal life. If we follow his "way," we will come to know the "truth" and will have "life," both here on earth as well as in Heaven.

In contrast, the devil hides his path in glamour or darkness; it is a deception that leads to death of bodies and souls, both in this lifetime and the next, in eternal torment and separation from God.

A Lifetime of Free Will Choices Form Our Pathways to Eternity

Our Choices Lead Us Along a Path of Our Own Free Will

Eternal Torment & Death with Satan ← Death • Deception • Path Disguised by Darkness or Glamour • **Choice/ Free Will** • The way • The Truth • The Life → Eternal Life with God through Jesus

Over time, our previous choices make us predisposed to recognizing Jesus' voice or not, following the Truth or not.

Every day, and too many times to count in a day, we make choices in our lives. The choices may be so seemingly small that we do not even notice them, or they may be so large that we need to think about them for a time before we make them. *Many* of these choices lead us on a path that is either toward God or away from him.

> Make known to me your ways, LORD;
> **teach me your paths.**
> Guide me by your fidelity and teach me,
> for you are God my savior,
> for you I wait all the day long.
> (Psalm 25:4-5)

It is not always easy to see that our choices, one after another, form a path. However, if we look at our lives or the lives of others in hindsight, we can see that the choices we have made lead us on a path toward the light of God or toward the darkness of the evil one. We can see that early small choices lead invariably to larger ones along the same path, unless there is some intervening event to change the direction. The path we are on does not dictate our final destination, but it does have a way of limiting our future choices.

For example, if someone drops out of high school, it will limit their choices with regard to college or career unless they take active steps to seek additional education. Similarly, some people talk about marijuana as being a "gateway" drug, meaning that people who begin taking marijuana early in life may be more likely, but not destined, to try more serious illegal drugs later in their lives. On the other hand, a person who desires to be a doctor will need to make many choices along the way as to the education and activities that support that goal.

In regard to our final, eternal destination, choices that are meant to satisfy our own desires may not always consider those of others or leave God out of the picture. They can change our paths or limit our ability to make other choices. Posting hurtful comments about others online, deciding not to go to church and pray with others in a community, or choosing to get a divorce for convenient purposes, all push us farther down a path and make us more disposed to continue farther down that same path.

St. Paul tells us clearly that we will either become slaves to sin or slaves to righteousness. The path we choose to follow is of our own free will.

> Do you not know that if you present yourselves to someone as obedient slaves, you are slaves of the one you obey, either of sin, which leads to death, or of obedience, which leads to righteousness? But thanks be to God that, although you were once slaves of sin, you have become obedient from the heart to the pattern of teaching to which you were entrusted. Freed from sin, you have become slaves of righteousness. (Romans 6:16-18)

God wants us to take a path to holiness. He lays out the clear path in his teachings, even though we do not always understand them. He wants all of us to follow his voice and be saved. He knows everything about us, and is still always willing to offer encouragement for us to turn back to him and be saved for all eternity.

> The LORD said to Moses, "Speak to the whole assembly and tell them: Be holy, for I the LORD your God, am holy." (Leviticus 19:1-2)

> [Moses spoke to the people, saying:] "This day the LORD, your God, is commanding you to observe these statutes and ordinances. Be careful, then, to observe them with your whole heart and with your whole being. Today you have accepted the LORD's agreement: ***he will be your God, and you will walk in his ways, observe his statutes, commandments, and ordinances, and obey his voice.***" (Deuteronomy 26:16-17)

> The law of the LORD is perfect,
> refreshing the soul.
> The decrees of the LORD is trustworthy,
> giving wisdom to the simple.
> (Psalm 19:8)

> Yet even now—oracle of the LORD—
> > return to me with your whole heart,
> > with fasting, weeping, and mourning.
> Rend your hearts, not your garments,
> > and return to the LORD, your God,
> For he is gracious and merciful,
> > slow to anger, abounding in steadfast love,
> > and relenting in punishment.
> (Joel 2:12-13)

The devil and, in many ways, our culture, tempt us, deceive us, and lead us away from the voice and path of God. Thoughts and messages of "everyone is doing it," "it's not that bad," or "it's my choice," surround and confront us. When we choose to follow the path of the evil one, we become his, as it is written:

> You belong to your father the devil and you willingly carry out your father's desires. He was a murderer from the beginning and does not stand in truth, because there is no truth in him. When he tells a lie, he speaks in character, because he is a liar and the father of lies. (John 8:44)

God Will Not Tempt Us to Evil

It is a choice. There is no temptation toward evil from God.

> Blessed is the man who perseveres in temptation, for when he has been proved he will receive the crown of life that he promised to those who love him. No one experiencing temptation should say,

> "I am being tempted by God"; for God is not subject to temptation to evil, and he himself tempts no one. Rather, each person is tempted when he is lured and enticed by his own desire. Then desire conceives and brings forth sin, and when sin reaches maturity it gives birth to death. (James 1:12-15)

All the choices we make of our own free will prepare us and teach us to see and recognize Jesus and his voice at that final moment.

> Do not be deceived, my beloved brothers: all good giving and every perfect gift is from above, coming down from the Father of lights, with whom there is no alteration or shadow caused by change. He willed to give us birth by the word of truth that we may be a kind of first fruits of his creatures. (James 1:16-18)

The Final Test

In our familiar recitation of the Lord's Prayer, in the last line, we pray: "and deliver us from evil." However, if we look at the translations and wording from both Matthew and Luke, we find that Jesus speaks of a "final test."

> [Jesus said:] "This is how you are to pray:
> Our Father in heaven,
>   hallowed be your name,
>   your kingdom come,
>   your will be done,
>   on earth as in heaven.
>   Give us today our daily bread;
>   and forgive us our debts,
>   as we forgive our debtors;
>   and ***do not subject us to the final test,***
>   but deliver us from the evil one.
> (Matthew 6:9-13)

> [Jesus] said to them, "When you pray, say:
> Father, hallowed be your name,
> > your kingdom come.
> > Give us each day our daily bread
> > and forgive us our sins
> > for we ourselves forgive everyone in debt to us,
> > and ***do not subject us to the final test***."
>
> (Luke 11:2-4)

Do not subject us to the final test. At the moment of death, we find ourselves along a great continuum from the brightest light of God in Heaven to the darkest depths of the Devil's Hell based upon the decisions we have made in our lifetimes and the paths we have chosen to follow. At that point, we are given one last final choice of Heaven or Hell – to be with God for eternity or to reject him and go with the devil.

The closer we are to the light, at the moment of death, the easier it will be for us to choose Heaven. The closer we are to the darkness, the easier it will be to make a final choice for Hell.

> Now this is the message that we have heard from him and proclaim to you: God is light, and in him there is no darkness at all. If we say, "We have fellowship with him," while we continue to walk in darkness, we lie and do not act in truth. But if we walk in the light as he is in the light, then we have fellowship with one another, and the blood of his Son Jesus cleanses us from all sin. If we say, "We are without sin," we deceive ourselves, and the truth is not in us. If we acknowledge our sins, he is faithful and just and will forgive our sins and cleanse us from every wrongdoing. If we say, "We have not sinned," we make him a liar, and his word is not in us. (1 John 1:5-10)

Catholic teaching, as well as my Adoration experience, and all the revelations of his love in the Bible, tell us that God loves and respects us so much that he has given us free will. It is God's true and pure love for us that has created us with the ability to choose our thoughts and actions. If we listen to the teachings of God and Jesus, we will be closer to him during our lifetimes and prepare ourselves to recognize Him when we make that final choice.

> ***The people who walked in darkness***
>   ***have seen a great light;***
> ***Upon those who lived in a land of gloom***
>   ***a light has shone.***
> You have brought them abundant joy
>   and great rejoicing;…
> For a child is born to us, a son is given to us;
>   upon his shoulder dominion rests.
> They name him Wonder-Counselor, God-Hero,
>   Father-Forever, Prince of Peace.
> His dominion is vast
>   and forever peaceful,…
> Upon David's throne, and over his kingdom,
>   which he confirms and sustains
> By judgment and justice,
>   both now and forever.
> The zeal of the LORD of hosts will do this!
> (Isaiah 9:1-2, 5-6)

The messages of God have been given to us. We have seen and heard them all our lives. It is our choice whether to walk in the path of light or be tempted along a path that leads to darkness and sin. We cannot say that we did not know. If we say that God did not tell us, we are ignoring all the prophets and the life, death and resurrection of his only Son, Jesus. As God told the prophet Jeremiah:

> I gave them no command concerning burnt offering or sacrifice. This rather is what I commanded them: Listen to my voice; then I will be your God and you shall be my people. Walk exactly in the way I command you, so that you may prosper.
>
> But they did not listen to me, nor did they pay attention. They walked in the stubbornness of their evil hearts and ***turned their backs, not their faces, to me***. From the day that your ancestors left the land of Egypt even to this day, ***I kept on sending all my servants the prophets to you. Yet they have not listened to me nor have they paid attention***. (Jeremiah 7:22-26)

However, we can choose to see and hear. We can choose to turn from evil and toward the Lord, and we can choose to turn our faces to God. Then, we shall be in the light.

> ***If you return to the Almighty, you will be restored***;
>   if you put iniquity far from your tent,
> Then the Almighty himself shall be your gold
>   and your sparkling silver.
> ***For then you shall delight in the Almighty,
>   you shall lift up your face toward God.***
> (Job 22:23, 25-26)

Continuum from the Light of Heaven to the Darkness of Hell

This continuum represents our choices at the moment of death. Where we enter the continuum is dependent upon the choices we have made in life. Where we spend eternity, Heaven or Hell, is dependent upon our final choice.

Our actions, during our life on earth, determine how clearly we see and hear Jesus and how close we already are to Heaven. In that

Continuum from the Light of Heaven to the Darkness of Hell

God, Jesus, Heaven, Pure Light

Clear, Bright — Souls who are closest to God when they die. They easily recognize Him, his voice and his Mother. While these souls have free will to choose, they only desire their place with God.

Misty — Souls here know Jesus' voice and willingly desire to atone for their earthly wrong-doings. Jesus is in a mist since the souls here could not bear the true light of Christ without first atoning for sins. Higher levels of Purgatory – souls progress from here toward the light of Heaven.

Foggy, Gray — Souls here still recognize God and desire to be with Him but are removed from him by earthly sin. Deepest levels of Purgatory – much suffering because souls feel separated from God during their period of atonement.

Dark, Hidden Torment — Souls here do not readily recognize Jesus' voice nor do they purposely reject Him. The Devil tempts them with lies – "you don't need him." The evil one deceives them into rejecting the need to atone for earthly sins. Souls here would enter the highest level of Hell if they do not ultimately follow Jesus.

Souls who reject God and blame him for their state of being. As souls progress farther into Hell, they "rage against God and become like beasts."

Darkest Night — Deepest levels of Hell – darkest eternal torment.

Hell

Jesus is the Way, the Truth and the Life ↑

The Deceptions of the Evil One ↓

final moment, Jesus will be like the star of Bethlehem to guide us to our eternal home. How brightly we see and recognize the star is dependent upon the choices we make during our lifetimes and how much we desire to be with God for eternity.

The farther that we have strayed from God's path in our lifetime, the darker our state at the moment of death. The darker our state, the harder it will be to see and recognize the Son, Jesus, and the harder the choice for Heaven will be because the devil will be there trying to deceive our souls into Hell.

God is pure, clear brightness. As mortals, we would never be able to see the face of God without our destruction except for the love of God. Think of the sun. If we get too close to the sun, we will burn up. Even being in the desert without shelter would cause us to die of exposure to the sun in a matter of days. Then think of the sun on a foggy or misty day. We still know that the sun is there because of the light behind the clouds, but it is not nearly as clear, nor hot.

Our earthly sun is simply our closest star. We can see the brightness of other stars in the night sky, but they are farther away, and it is hard to pick out individual stars unless they are especially bright or we have studied the constellations. The night stars do not provide the same level of light and comfort as our day star, and while they may be a guide for nighttime travel, it is far less easy to understand their movements in the sky than it is to understand the earth's movements relative to the sun.

Taking this analogy, in our final moment, we will find ourselves along a continuum of light from the brightest light of Heaven to the darkest depths of Hell based upon the paths we have chosen to pursue during our lifetimes.

Regardless of the place where we enter the continuum, Jesus will be there to guide us to Heaven. However, where we enter the continuum will determine how clear and visible Jesus is for us. If we have lived our lives close to Jesus, he will be readily recognizable, like our day sun. But if we have lived our lives farther away from Jesus, and tempted away by the evil one, it will be harder to recognize him because we will be in the midst of fog or darkness, and Jesus will be among other voices trying to lead us in a different direction.

If we choose God and Heaven, we will readily encounter Jesus and his Mother, Mary, like the Magi did in the story of the Epiphany. The word, "epiphany," in fact, has come to mean a new understanding. Like the Magi, we first need to recognize the light of Jesus. We need to see that he is the way, the truth and our very life. We need to follow His way and, as our final act of free will, do him homage.

> And behold, the star that they had seen at its rising preceded them, until it came and stopped over the place where the child was. They were overjoyed at seeing the star, and on entering the house they saw the child with Mary his mother. They prostrated themselves and did him homage. (Matthew 2:9-11)

In the Adoration event that I experienced, I understood that Mary was right by Jesus' side in the battle for the soul. Both Jesus and Mary were terribly pained by the soul that was walking away from Jesus. In our lives, they are with us always to encourage us according to God's laws and along His paths.

> But when the fullness of time had come, God sent his Son, born of a woman, born under the law, to ransom those under the law, so that we might receive adoption. As proof that you are children, God sent the spirit of his Son into our hearts, crying out, "Abba, Father!" So you are no longer a slave but a child, and if a child then also an heir, through God. (Galatians 4:4-7)

Jesus explains that the continuum ranges from the resurrection of life down to an afterlife of condemnation. At our death, everyone will hear the voice of Jesus and *those who hear and respond to him will live.*

> Jesus answered and said to them, "Amen, amen, I say to you, a son cannot do anything on his own, but only what he sees his father doing; for what he does, his son will do also. For the Father loves his Son and shows him everything that he himself does, and he will show him greater works than these, so that you may be amazed. For just as the Father raises the dead and gives life, so also does the Son give life to whomever he wishes. Nor does the Father judge anyone, but he has given all judgment to his Son, so that all may honor the Son just as they honor the Father. Whoever does not honor the Son does not honor the Father who sent him. *Amen, amen, I say to you, whoever hears my word and believes in the one who sent me has eternal life and will not come to condemnation, but has passed from death to life.* Amen, amen, I say to you, the hour is coming and is now here when the dead will hear the voice of the Son of God, and *those who hear will live.* For just as the Father has life in himself, so also he gave to his Son the possession of life in himself. And he gave him power to exercise judgment, because he is the Son of Man. Do not be amazed at this, because the hour is coming in which all who are in the tombs *will hear his voice and will come out, those who have done good deeds to the resurrection of life*, but those who have done wicked deeds to the resurrection of condemnation.

> "I cannot do anything on my own; I judge as I hear, and my judgment is just, because I do not seek my own will but the will of the one who sent me."

(John 5:19-30)

If we look at the continuum, those who have chosen a path closest to Jesus during their lifetimes – whom we may choose to call saints or saintly – will be closest to the light upon their deaths. They are in the bright white radiance of Christ. While they still retain their free will to choose Heaven or Hell, they have long ago chosen to take their place with God for all eternity. For these individuals, it is like seeing the sun on the brightest clearest day, there is no doubt of its light and warmth and the life it brings. They recognize Jesus and Mary immediately, they have died in a state of pure grace, which can only be granted by God.

A little farther down the continuum, there are souls who have followed the Lord's way in their lives but have passed with some stain of unconfessed or unrepentant sin upon their souls. Depending upon the degree of those sins, these souls will find themselves in a mist or fog-like state. They still clearly recognize Jesus as Lord, but because they will immediately recognize the harm that their sins have caused, they are not able to look upon the Lord directly. They recognize the need for their atonement of sin and welcome the blessing of Purgatory. Purgatory is a pure gift from God because it allows us an opportunity to make up for things we could have, should have, or have done in our lives that has put distance between us and God.

These souls are in a mist or fog because they are unable to endure the direct pure light of God without first atoning for their sins. While the evil one will make one last attempt to deceive them, these souls are close enough to God that they will recognize the deceptions for what they truly are and reject the snares of the Devil.

Once they have elected to be with God for eternity and desire to make up for their earthly sins in Purgatory, they enter an appropriate level of Purgatory based upon their level of sins. Suffering in Purgatory is related to distance from God upon death, the desire to be with him, and for the harm we have caused or chosen in our lives.

It is important to note, that once a soul enters Purgatory, it is saved. Its ultimate destination is Heaven, and nothing can change that. That is why the Catholic Church refers to these souls as "holy souls." We can and should pray for the holy souls in Purgatory to help them achieve their true goal of being eternally with God. As St. Paul tells us:

> I give thanks to my God at every remembrance of you, praying always with joy in my every prayer for all of you, because of your partnership for the gospel from the first day until now. I am confident of this, ***that the one who began a good work in you will continue to complete it until the day of Christ Jesus***. It is right that I should think this way about all of you, because I hold you in my heart, you who are all partners with me in grace, both in my imprisonment and in the defense and confirmation of the gospel. For God is my witness, how I long for all of you with the affection of Christ Jesus. And this is my prayer: that your love may increase ever more and more in knowledge and every kind of perception, to discern what is of value, ***so that you may be pure and blameless for the day of Christ***, filled with the fruit of righteousness that comes through Jesus Christ for the glory and praise of God. (Philippians 1:3-11)

God will continue his good work in us until we become "pure and blameless" and are completely healed of all sin for the "day of Christ Jesus."

> See what love the Father has bestowed on us that we may be called the children of God. Yet so we are. The reason the world does not know us is that it did not know him. Beloved, we are God's children now; what we shall be has not yet been revealed. We do know that when it is revealed we shall be like him, for we shall see him as he is. Everyone who has this hope based on him makes himself pure, as he is pure. (1 John 3:1-3)

Farther down the continuum, are souls farther into the darkness of the evil one. These souls have chosen to follow the temptations of the evil one during their lifetimes. Jesus and Mary will be there for them upon their deaths, as they battle for the eternal salvation of every soul, but since these souls have followed the ways of the evil one in their lifetimes, and have not repented of their sins, they are farther away from the Lord and farther in the darkness. The previous choices of these souls have likened Jesus to a star in the night sky. While Jesus is there to guide them to Heaven, he is more distant from the soul and harder to recognize.

> To this day, in fact, whenever Moses is read, a veil lies over their hearts, but whenever a person turns to the Lord the veil is removed. Now the Lord is the Spirit, and where the Spirit of the Lord is, there is freedom. All of us, gazing with unveiled face on the glory of the Lord, are being transformed into the same image from glory to glory, as from the Lord who is the Spirit.

> Therefore, since we have this ministry through the mercy shown us, we are not discouraged.

> And even though *our gospel is veiled, it is veiled for those who are perishing*, in whose case the god of this age has blinded the minds of the unbelievers.

(2 Corinthians 3:15-18, 4:1, 3-4)

The evil one will be there with temptations. His temptations, most likely, will be of the guilty pleasures that appealed to us in our earthly lives. He will deceive. Jesus can only tell the truth. God cannot lie. The souls in this farther darkness still have one more chance of Heaven. They need only to recognize Jesus as Lord, repent of their earthly sins and accept the need for atonement. Then they will belong to the Lord eternally. This is a tenuous spot because they have trained themselves to listen to and respond to the voice of the evil one during their lifetimes. They have trained themselves to reject the path and ways of the Lord, and may have come to feel bitter toward God and his ways. They may have trained themselves to blame God or others for anything they feel has been unjust in their lives.

> Everyone who commits sin commits lawlessness, for sin is lawlessness. You know that he was revealed to take away sins, and in him there is no sin. No one who remains in him sins; no one who sins has seen him or known him. (1 John 3:4-6)

Even when we do sin, God has sent his son to take away our sins, if we only ask.

> My children, I am writing this to you so that you may not commit sin. But if anyone does sin, we have an Advocate with the Father, Jesus Christ the righteous one. He is expiation for our sins, and not for our sins only but for those of the whole world. (1 John 2:1-2)

It is ultimately the soul's choice. Jesus will meet any soul wherever it is, no matter the circumstances. If this soul simply reaches out to find Jesus' voice and chooses his path at the end, even though it finds itself in the darkness of the evil one and of the night, it will be on the path to Heaven.

However, if the soul continues to listen to the deceptions of the evil one, and rejects the need to atone for earthly sins, it will find itself on a path to eternal darkness in Hell.

The Writing in Our Hearts

Where we stand in our final moment, and how prepared we are at that moment, is not dependent upon ritualistic sacrifices as much as it is something found in our innermost being. In the letter to the Hebrews, we are told that, with the coming of Jesus, the law of the Lord has been written on the hearts of all souls by the Holy Spirit.

> For this reason, when he came into the world, he said:
> ***"This is the covenant I will establish with them after those days, says the Lord:***
> ***'I will put my laws in their hearts,***
> ***and I will write them upon their minds,'"***
>
> he also says:
> "Their sins and their evildoing
> I will remember no more."
>
> Where there is forgiveness of these, there is no longer offering for sin.
> (Hebrews 10:5, 16-18)

Jesus, through his death and resurrection became the one sacrificial offering for the atonement of all sins. Through this offering, ritualistic sacrifices are no longer necessary, but we must have a repentant heart for our sins. When we truly repent of our sins, they will be forgiven.

Now that we know the law is written upon our hearts and minds, it is up to each of us to help one another to be true to it. Some may ask about the people in the world who have never even heard about Jesus; we now know that the truth of God is written on their hearts and minds as well. Jesus will meet them wherever they are in their lives, just as he does for people who contemplate his words day and night.

Whether we have formal teaching of God or not, truth remains. Sin is evident by its works and consequences. The evil one tempts us to justify sin – "everyone does it," "it's not that bad," it's a victimless crime." In our hearts we know that sin is wrong. We also know what is good and right.

> We must consider how to rouse one another to love and good works. We should not stay away from our assembly, as is the custom of some, but encourage one another, and this all the more as you see the day drawing near.
>
> If we sin deliberately after receiving knowledge of the truth, there no longer remains sacrifice for sins but a fearful prospect of judgment and a flaming fire that is going to consume the adversaries.
>
> (Hebrews 10:24-27)

The Ten Commandments

What then, is the law that is written on our hearts and in our minds. We all know that God gave the Ten Commandments to Moses. We can probably recite at least a few of the do's and don'ts. "Thou shall not steal," "thou shall not kill," may come to mind first.

While the actual words are more complex, however, in summary, the Ten Commandments are:

1. I am the Lord, your God; you shall not have strange gods before me.

2. You shall not take the name of the Lord, your God, in vain.
3. Remember to keep holy the Lord's day.
4. Honor your father and mother.
5. You shall not kill.
6. You shall not commit adultery.
7. You shall not steal.
8. You shall not bear false witness against your neighbor.
9. You shall not covet (desire, crave) your neighbor's wife.
10. You shall not covet your neighbor's goods.

Life and Death, the Blessing and the Curse

When Moses gave the Commandments to the people, he explained that God intended the Commandments to be more than a set of arbitrary rules, he explained that they were a way of life that is good, not evil, and a road map to the promised land.

> See, ***I have today set before you life and good, death and evil***. (Deuteronomy 30:15)

If we think of the "promised land" as eternal life in Heaven, and death as death in Hell, we can see the roadmap more clearly. Once the Commandments were given to us, we can no longer say that we did not know, we did not understand. That is why the Commandments are said to be a blessing and a curse. They are a blessing because God has given us the way that is good and leads to Heaven. They are a curse, because, knowing the path, if we choose to stray and serve the evil one, we will perish.

> If you obey the commandments of the LORD, your God, which I am giving you today, loving the LORD, your God, and walking in his ways, and keeping his commandments, statutes and ordinances, you will live and grow numerous, and the LORD, your God, will bless you in the land you are entering to possess. If, however, your heart turns away and you do not obey, but are led astray

and bow down to other gods and serve them, I tell you today that you will certainly perish; you will not have a long life on the land which you are crossing the Jordan to enter and possess. I call heaven and earth today to witness against you: *I have set before you life and death, the blessing and the curse. Choose life, then, that you and your descendants may live, by loving the LORD, your God, obeying his voice, and holding fast to him.* (Deuteronomy 30:16-19)

Fulfillment of the Commandments

Jesus tells us, that the Commandments given to us by God, through Moses, are still as relevant today as they were thousands of years ago. Jesus, in his teaching, continually points us back to the path laid out for us by God, through Moses, and to all the messages of the prophets. We cannot say that God is silent. He has been speaking to us through all of written history. He continues to speak to us today through his words and teachings.

Jesus tells us:

> "Do not think that I have come to abolish the law or the prophets. *I have come not to abolish but to fulfill. Amen, I say to you, until heaven and earth pass away, not the smallest letter or the smallest part of a letter will pass from the law, until all things have taken place.* Therefore, whoever breaks one of the least of these commandments and teaches others to do so will be called least in the kingdom of heaven. But whoever obeys and teaches these commandments will be called greatest in the kingdom of heaven." (Matthew 5:17-19)

It is our life's work, not only to follow the path of God, but to teach it to others. We are meant to pass the teachings to our children and their children. We are meant to give the gift of good and of eternal life to as many people as we can find, as many people as will listen. Also, we are meant to teach others by our actions. Remember:

> The law of the LORD is perfect,
>   refreshing the soul.
> The decrees of the LORD is trustworthy,
>   giving wisdom to the simple.
> (Psalm 19:8)

The Parable of the Rich Man and Lazarus

The story of the rich man and Lazarus has so many things to tell us about how the choices we make in this life will lead to our final destination after death.

> "There was a rich man who dressed in purple garments and fine linen and dined sumptuously each day. And lying at his door was a poor man named Lazarus, covered with sores, who would gladly have eaten his fill of the scraps that fell from the rich man's table. Dogs even used to come and lick his sores. When the poor man died, he was carried away by angels to the bosom of Abraham. The rich man also died and was buried, and from the netherworld, where he was in torment, he raised his eyes and saw Abraham far off and Lazarus at his side. And he cried out, 'Father Abraham, have pity on me. Send Lazarus to dip the tip of his finger in water and cool my tongue, for I am suffering torment in these flames.' Abraham replied, 'My child, remember that you received what was good during your lifetime while Lazarus likewise received what was bad; but now he is comforted here, whereas you are tormented.

Moreover, between us and you a great chasm is established to prevent anyone from crossing who might wish to go from our side to yours or from your side to ours.' He said, 'Then I beg you, father, send him to my father's house, for I have five brothers, so that he may warn them, lest they too come to this place of torment.' But Abraham replied, '*They have Moses and the prophets. Let them listen to them.*' He said, '*Oh no, father Abraham, but if someone from the dead goes to them, they will repent.*' Then Abraham said, '*If they will not listen to Moses and the prophets, neither will they be persuaded if someone should rise from the dead.*'"

(Luke 16:19-31)

The rich man in this story clearly had been taught the law of God. We know this because he does not disagree with Abraham that he has heard from Moses and the prophets. He only says that these messages were not enough for him to change his ways and to believe. He heard, and may have even believed that he was following the law and teachings of Moses and the prophets during his lifetime.

What, then, is the rich man's sin? How did he end up in Hell? The rich man does not harm Lazarus, he does not kill him, he simply ignores him and his plight. He has not directly disobeyed a commandment when it comes to Lazarus, but he passes close by him and steps over him to enter or to exit his door. What made him step over Lazarus every day? Was it fear, or just lack of love and compassion?

Like Ebenezer Scrooge in Charles Dickens', "A Christmas Carol," the rich man is focused on his own business or busy-ness and does not believe he needs to pay attention to that of anyone else.

However, the choices he made during his life had led him away from the choice of Heaven and into the torment of Hell.

What about us? Could we possibly be as guilty as the rich man? As readers of the Gospels we do have an advantage over the rich man in the story. Not only do we know the teaching of Moses and prophets, we have the messages of Christ, the Son of God who has risen from the dead. Will we be ***persuaded by the someone who has risen from the dead?***

The story is clearly about our choices in this life. How many times do we pass by someone close enough to touch and then pass on by? Who is at our door? How do we respond to the elderly friend, or sick parent, starving child on the other side of the world, or beggar on the street?

And, it is not just an individual effort. How do we, as a community, care for our people in need? I look at the homeless crisis in our country right now and I see Lazarus in my mind. How many of us drive by the homeless daily on our way to our safe and secure offices, workplaces or homes? What are we doing to serve our fellow men and women? What are we doing to secure solutions and demand justice?

This story is not just about the punishment of the rich man, but about the love of God that has come to save us all. God loved us so much that he sent his Son to save us. He is pure love, and when we have love, we will follow God to Heaven. When we truly love God, we will make the right choices in this life so that we will not primarily live in fear of punishment, but rather, will love one another all the way to Heaven.

> Beloved, if God so loved us, we also must love one another. No one has ever seen God. Yet, if we love one another, God remains in us, and his love is brought to perfection in us.

This is how we know that we remain in him and he in us, that he has given us of his Spirit. Moreover, we have seen and testify that the Father sent his Son as savior of the world. Whoever acknowledges that Jesus is the Son of God, God remains in him and he in God. We have come to know and to believe in the love God has for us.

God is love, and whoever remains in love remains in God and God in him. In this is love brought to perfection among us, that we have confidence on the day of judgment because as he is, so are we in this world. There is no fear in love, but perfect love drives out fear because fear has to do with punishment, and so one who fears is not yet perfect in love. We love because he first loved us. If anyone says, "I love God," but hates his brother, he is a liar; for whoever does not love a brother whom he has seen cannot love God whom he has not seen. This is the commandment we have from him: whoever loves God must also love his brother.

Everyone who believes that Jesus is the Christ is begotten by God, and everyone who loves the father loves the one begotten by him. In this way we know that we love the children of God when we love God and obey his commandments. For the love of God is this, that we keep his commandments. And his commandments are not burdensome, for whoever is begotten by God conquers the world. And the victory that conquers the world is our faith.

(1 John 4:11-5:4)

This is the message that is written on our hearts.

The Analogy of the Garden

I do not remember where I first heard the analogy of God putting people in the garden of our lives, but I think of it often, and I have told it to my daughters many, many times. Often when they are struggling with someone in their lives, I tell them that God has put that person in their garden for a reason. I tell them, sometimes that person is in your garden so that you can tend to them, and sometimes they are in your garden so that they can tend to you. Some people will be in your garden for only a season, some will be in your garden for your lifetime.

I believe that analogy is about looking at the people around us with love, whether they seem to be a beautiful flower or even when they feel like a thorn or a weed. I promise you that right now you are a flower or a weed in someone else's garden and I promise you that one time or another God has put a flower, or a wilting plant, or a weed, or even a Lazarus in your garden. How well are you tending to the garden that God has given to you? Look around, is there someone who needs tending in your garden that you are not seeing or are choosing to pass by?

The Purpose of the Parables

Jesus often spoke in parables to the disciples and the crowds. There are two parables that specifically reflect this analogy of the garden to me. The first is the Parable of the Sower, and the second is the Parable of the Wheat. I would like to explore these two parables within the context of the analogy of the garden.

Often, when we have heard these two parables, or have heard others reflect on them, even our priests when giving homilies, we are likely to think of how they relate to our own selves. At another level, they are also about how we are to tend the garden of the Lord; to help others grow closer to God and, by doing so, grow closer to God ourselves.

The tradition of using parables to convey complex spiritual messages is used throughout the Bible. Much as we might use a story with exaggerated characters to explain an important truth or teaching to children, the use of parables shares a truth about God in human terms. In Psalm 78, God tells the Prophet Asaph:

> ***Attend, my people, to my teaching;***
> ***listen to the words of my mouth.***
> ***I will open my mouth in a parable,***
> ***unfold the puzzling events of the past.***
> What we have heard and know;
> things our ancestors have recounted to us.
> We do not keep them from our children;
> we recount them to the next generation.
> That the next generation might come to know,
> children yet to be born.
> In turn they were to recount them to their children,
> that they too might put their confidence in God,
> And not forget God's deeds,
> but keep his commandments.
> They were not to be like their ancestors,
> a rebellious and defiant generation,
> A generation whose heart was not constant,
> and whose spirit was not faithful to God.
> (Psalm 78:1-4, 6-8)

In Matthew Chapter 13, Jesus explains why he speaks in Parables. The parables are a way of understanding that which cannot be easily understood by human minds - the mysteries of God's kingdom. Like the analogy of the garden, we must look deeply into the parable to receive their riches.

> The disciples approached him [Jesus] and said, "Why do you speak to them in parables?" He said to them in reply, "Because knowledge of the mysteries of the kingdom of heaven has been grant-

> ed to you, but to them it has not been granted. ***To anyone who has, more will be given and he will grow rich; from anyone who has not, even what he has will be taken away***. This is why I speak to them in parables, because 'they look but do not see and hear but do not listen or understand.'
> (Matthew 13:10-13)

Jesus tells the parables so that people not only see themselves in them, but also so that we will make a change in our lives and help others to make a change in theirs. He wants us to hear the messages, not simply the words. He wants everyone to "see with their eyes and hear with their ears and understand with their hearts and be converted," so that we, and others, may be healed.

What can Jesus mean when he says: "To anyone who has, more will be given and he will grow rich; from anyone who has not, even what he has will be taken away?"

If we use the analogy of the garden, it can mean that those who really understand the messages of the parables will "grow rich," not only in their own understanding or their personal benefit, but in opportunities to share this understanding with others.

> Peter began to say to him, "We have given up everything and followed you." Jesus said, "Amen, I say to you, there is no one who has given up house or brothers or sisters or mother or father or children or lands for my sake and for the sake of the gospel who will not receive a hundred times more now in this present age: houses and brothers and sisters and mothers and children and lands, with persecutions, and eternal life in the age to come."
> (Mark 10:28-30)

Jesus tells us, that when we begin to tend to others in our garden, we will receive back "a hundred times more now in this present age," including "brothers and sisters and mothers and children." We will receive more to tend in our garden.

If we learn to "hear with our ears," and "understand with our hearts," we will learn how to live for the "sake of the Gospel." We will learn how not to live for the things of this world, but rather for the people of the world, especially the people in our own lives, the people in our own garden. Then we will be living and helping them to live for "eternal life in the age to come." It is what we give up now, how we live now, that will guide us there.

We are also told by Jesus, however, that we can no longer say we did not know or understand. That is because He has given us the riches of the "mysteries of the kingdom of heaven." This is a blessing to be sure.

> "But blessed are your eyes, because they see, and your ears, because they hear. Amen, I say to you, many prophets and righteous people longed to see what you see but did not see it, and to hear what you hear but did not hear it." (Matthew 13:16-17)

Not everyone has had the opportunity to "see" and "hear" the good news. This gift brings, not only an opportunity, but also an obligation, to love those in our garden and to share the words of Jesus. When we follow the words and actions of Jesus, we will "see" their wounds and "hear" their sorrows, and act to help them out of love.

As St. Paul tells us in his most famous discourse on love, unless we act out of love, we have done nothing.

> If I speak in human and angelic tongues but do not have love, I am a resounding gong or a clashing cymbal. ***And if I have the gift of prophecy and comprehend all mysteries and all knowledge; if I have all faith so as to move mountains but do not have love, I am nothing.*** If I give away everything

> I own, and if I hand my body over so that I may boast but do not have love, I gain nothing.
>
> Love is patient, love is kind. It is not jealous, [love] is not pompous, it is not inflated, it is not rude, it does not seek its own interests, it is not quick-tempered, it does not brood over injury, it does not rejoice over wrongdoing but rejoices with the truth. It bears all things, believes all things, hopes all things, endures all things.
>
> Love never fails. If there are prophecies, they will be brought to nothing; if tongues, they will cease; if knowledge, it will be brought to nothing. For we know partially and we prophesy partially, but when the perfect comes, the partial will pass away. When I was a child, I used to talk as a child, think as a child, reason as a child; when I became a man, I put aside childish things. At present we see indistinctly, as in a mirror, but then face to face. At present I know partially; then I shall know fully, as I am fully known. ***So faith, hope, love remain, these three; but the greatest of these is love.***
>
> (1 Corinthians 13:1-13)

The Parable of the Sower

The Parable of the Sower is a familiar bible story. It is a story that is told to us from an early age; it is even found in many children's bible story books.

> On that day, Jesus went out of the house and sat down by the sea. Such large crowds gathered around him that he got into a boat and sat down, and the whole crowd stood along the shore. And he spoke to them at length in parables, saying: "A sower went out to sow. And as he sowed, some

> seed fell on the path, and birds came and ate it up. Some fell on rocky ground, where it had little soil. It sprang up at once because the soil was not deep, and when the sun rose it was scorched, and it withered for lack of roots. Some seed fell among thorns, and the thorns grew up and choked it. But some seed fell on rich soil, and produced fruit, a hundred or sixty or thirtyfold. Whoever has ears ought to hear." (Matthew 13:1-9)

Later, when the disciples asked Jesus about this parable, he explained:

> "Hear then the parable of the sower. The seed sown on the path is the one who hears the word of the kingdom without understanding it, and the evil one comes and steals away what was sown in his heart. The seed sown on rocky ground is the one who hears the word and receives it at once with joy. But he has no root and lasts only for a time. When some tribulation or persecution comes because of the word, he immediately falls away. The seed sown among thorns is the one who hears the word, but then worldly anxiety and the lure of riches choke the word and it bears no fruit. But the seed sown on rich soil is the one who hears the word and understands it, who indeed bears fruit and yields a hundred or sixty or thirtyfold." (Matthew 13:18-23)

A common way of explaining this Gospel is for the priest in his homily to ask where we "fall" in the story. Has the word of God fallen on our heart and landed on the walking path, or rocky ground, or among thorns, or rich soil? Has God's word taken root in our heart or has the evil one stolen it away?

While that is a perfectly excellent question and message, let us focus on the very last line. "But the seed sown on rich soil is the one who hears the word and understands it, ***who indeed bears fruit and yields a hundred or sixty or thirtyfold.***"

Assuming our hearts are "rich soil" for a moment, how would we go about bearing fruit and yielding a hundred or sixty or thirtyfold? How would we go about spreading the word of God to bring one hundred souls to God, or even just one? If we think of our lives as a garden and we are the gardeners, the parable yields even more.

The walking path is hard, beaten down soil. We all know people, and maybe even ourselves, whose lives have been hard and they are beaten down by the circumstances of life. For these people, even if the word of God is put in front of them, it is snatched away so quickly that they hardly even know it was there. How can we help to break up that soil for them, make the road a bit easier for them? Can we babysit for the single mom who never gets a moment for herself? Or even just place a gift under the Christmas Giving Tree? Can we sit with someone and just listen and explain that we understand and love them?

We also know people who feel betrayed in life – the people on rocky ground. These are the people that down deep in their hearts desperately want to believe, but push faith away because they feel they have been betrayed and they need to protect themselves. For these people, something has "scorched" their belief in God. It may be the people who have been abused by a priest or scout leader or relative early in their lives. It may be people who have been neglected or abused by a parent or the social services system. In our role as gardener when they come into our lives, how can we help to rebuild that trust? Can we listen to their stories and help them to understand and believe that Jesus wants to heal them? Can we take the time with them to help them build up trust and know that not everyone will hurt or abandon them?

What about the seed that fell among the thorns? These are the people born into poverty or violence or oppression. They may have had to resort to drugs or violence or illegal activities themselves because it is all they have ever known, or because they felt it was the only way to survive. They may be the people who have grown up among gangs, or oppressive foreign governments, or the girls or women who have had abortions because our culture told them "it was their bodies and their right to choose." The evil one speaks loudly in our culture. He desires these souls to be with him and continues to try to deceive them. How can we help these individuals understand that their choices are leading them away from the path of God and help them return to the path of light? Can we invite them to church with us? Can we act in a way that is stronger than words?

It is important to understand as well, that where we are in the story today is not where we always will be. If that were the case, there would be no need to yield a harvest. If you are among the weeds, or on the walking path, I pray that someone will tend to you in their garden and help you to find the rich, rich soil of God's mercy and love.

We may not be able to heal the physical ailments of those not in rich soil, or cure their former distress or memories, but we can make them feel valued, important and loved – especially loved by Jesus.

If we are blessed to be in the rich soil of the Gospel, even if we have previously been on rocky ground, or among thorns, or on the walking path along the way, it is our duty to tend the garden that God has given us, and to yield a harvest for the Lord. It takes courage to reach out to people who are sick or frightened or lonely or weak, but God has sent us the Holy Spirit to guide us and give us strength. We can do it! One soul at a time.

As Saint Francis of Assisi said, "Speak the Gospel at all times. Use words if you have to."

The Parable of the Weeds Among the Wheat

Next, Jesus tells a parable of the Weeds Among the Wheat. It is a story about God giving us chances right up to the moment of death.

> He [Jesus] proposed another parable to them. "The kingdom of heaven may be likened to a man who sowed good seed in his field. While everyone was asleep his enemy came and sowed weeds all through the wheat, and then went off. ***When the crop grew and bore fruit, the weeds appeared as well***. The slaves of the householder came to him and said, 'Master, did you not sow good seed in your field? Where have the weeds come from?' He answered, 'An enemy has done this.' His slaves said to him, 'Do you want us to go and pull them up?' He replied, 'No, if you pull up the weeds you might uproot the wheat along with them. Let them grow together until harvest; then at harvest time I will say to the harvesters, "First collect the weeds and tie them in bundles for burning; but gather the wheat into my barn."'"
>
> Then, dismissing the crowds, he went into the house. His disciples approached him and said, "Explain to us the parable of the weeds in the field." He said in reply, "He who sows good seed is the Son of Man, the field is the world, the good seed the children of the kingdom. The weeds are the children of the evil one, and the enemy who sows them is the devil. The harvest is the end of the age, and the harvesters are angels. Just as weeds are collected and burned [up] with fire, so will it be at the end of the age. The Son of Man will send his angels, and they will collect out of his kingdom all who cause others to sin and all evildoers. They

will throw them into the fiery furnace, where there will be wailing and grinding of teeth. Then the righteous will shine like the sun in the kingdom of their Father. Whoever has ears ought to hear."

(Matthew 24-32, 36-43)

Unlike actual wheat and weeds, we have a choice about who we are to become in our lifetimes. Jesus is patient and he will wait to see what we will decide.

No matter who we are, or what our circumstances, we are surrounded by both good seed and weeds. In our situation, there may be more or less of either, but they are there and we need to recognize them because they can influence who we ultimately become.

It has been said that the easiest way for the devil to do his work is for us not to believe he exists. He does exist, and he does seek the ruin of all souls. He is jealous of the Lord and wants to deprive the Lord of as many souls as possible.

As Jesus tells us, we can recognize the good crop from the weeds by the fruit that they bear:

> "A good tree does not bear rotten fruit, nor does a rotten tree bear good fruit. For every tree is known by its own fruit. For people do not pick figs from thornbushes, nor do they gather grapes from brambles. A good person out of the store of goodness in his heart produces good, but an evil person out of a store of evil produces evil; for from the fullness of the heart the mouth speaks." (Luke 6:43-45)

We must look in our own gardens and recognize the fruit around us for what it is. Look to the fruit of those in your garden. There are those that seek and find the good in everyone else. On the other hand, there are those that seek only the negative. They search for and see the bad in everything, they look for a reason to defile others.

While it is not our duty to judge others, we must use our minds to distinguish the fruit that is produced by the those around us in our garden and use our free will to guide our actions. We must stay close to those who seek for the positive, the light, in others. This will help us to seek the light ourselves. We must try to avoid those who seek the negative, the darkness, for they will end up leading us down a wrong path.

Like us, demons have free will. The angels in Hell have chosen to be there and to work against the Lord. By temptation and deception, the evil one tries to convince us to follow his path to destruction and Hell. It is our God-given blessing to choose, but we need to choose wisely.

When we wonder, how can any soul choose Hell, we can also wonder why anyone, including ourselves, choose to sin? Sin is the first step on the road to Hell. We need to remember that in any moment, through our choices, our vision may be clouded and we may not see Jesus or the devil for what they are. If Jesus were standing in front of us today in all his glory and the devil were to reveal his true self, would anyone really choose to follow the devil? However, that is not how the choices of this world work, nor is it how our last choice at the time of death will likely present itself.

For those who have chosen the path of Jesus as the Way and the Truth and the Life, they will be closest to the light upon their death and will clearly recognize Jesus and his voice. For those who have chosen the way of darkness in their lives, the darkness will surround them, and it will be difficult to recognize Jesus, although he will still be there giving the soul one final chance.

The devil, however, will be there also. A soul in darkness has trained himself, over his lifetime, to recognize the voice and temptations of the evil one. The farther into the darkness, the more likely the soul will be to follow the temptations of the evil one, all the way to Hell and to torment.

Blessed is the man who perseveres in temptation, for when he has been proved he will receive the crown of life that he promised to those who love him. No one experiencing temptation should say, "I am being tempted by God"; for God is not subject to temptation to evil, and he himself tempts no one. Rather, each person is tempted when he is lured and enticed by his own desire. Then desire conceives and brings forth sin, and **when sin reaches maturity it gives birth to death**.

Do not be deceived, my beloved brothers: all good giving and every perfect gift is from above, coming down from the Father of lights, with whom there is **no alteration or shadow caused by change**. He willed to give us birth by the word of truth that we may be a kind of firstfruits of his creatures.

(James 1:12-18)

Prayer to St. Michael the Archangel

It has been said that Saint Pope Leo XIII wrote the prayer to Saint Michael the Archangel after having a vision of the devil or demonic spirits. He ordered the prayer to be recited for the protection of souls.

> *Saint Michael the Archangel, defend us in battle, be our protection against the wickedness and snares of the devil. May God rebuke him we humbly pray; and do thou, O Prince of the Heavenly host, by the power of God, cast into Hell Satan and all the evil spirits who prowl about the world seeking the ruin of souls. Amen.*

May the soul reading this prayer right now be under your protection, Saint Michael, and may you be there to protect him/

her at the moment of death as well. As we pray in the Lord's Prayer, "lead us not into temptation, but deliver us from evil." Let us hope that we remember this prayer especially at the moment of our own death. Amen.

And while the parable of the weeds among the wheat warns us of the weeds around us, sown by the evil one, it also calls us to think of how the good seed is meant to grow and persist in this garden. Are we only to worry about safeguarding ourselves? God warned Ezekiel that he would hold him accountable if he did not warn others around him about the danger of sin. God would hold him accountable for the death of their souls.

> You, son of man—I have appointed you as a sentinel; when you hear a word from my mouth, you must warn them for me. When I say to the wicked, "You wicked, you must die," and you do not speak up to warn the wicked about their ways, they shall die in their sins, but I will hold you responsible for their blood. If, however, you warn the wicked to turn from their ways, but they do not, then they shall die in their sins, but you shall save your life. (Ezekiel 33:7-9)

God also says that he wants people to turn from their evil ways and be saved.

> As for you, son of man, say to your people: The justice of the just will not save them on the day they sin; the wickedness of the wicked will not bring about their downfall on the day they turn from their wickedness. No, the just cannot save their lives on the day they sin. Even though I say to the just that they shall surely live, if they, relying on their justice, do wrong, none of their just deeds shall be remembered; because of the wrong they

> have done, they shall die. And though I say to the wicked that they shall die, if they turn away from sin and do what is just and right— returning pledges, restoring stolen goods, walking by statutes that bring life, doing nothing wrong—they shall surely live; they shall not die. (Ezekiel 33:12-15)

Now we know. We cannot say that we do not know. We cannot say that we were not sent to tell and warn others. It is not enough to save our own souls.

As we watch our culture moving ever closer toward the darkness, we can see it with our own eyes. We see the statistics that the number of people who believe in God has been dropping. We watch on television, as an actress publicly states that her success was due to her abortion. We see homelessness and lawlessness and drug abuse and suicide become an epidemic and no one lifts a finger to help. This shows us that we must take up the fight, we must bring change to the world, one soul at a time. This is not only to save that soul, but our own.

Jesus Begins His Mission

It is an undeniably huge mission to save souls. What can we learn about our own mission in life from the way that Jesus started his ministry? It is never too early or too late to begin our mission. It is about the choices we make throughout our lives that bring us closer to or farther away from God at our final choice. It is about faith and words and actions.

After John the Baptist had been arrested, Jesus knew it was time for him to begin his mission to the world. Jesus began his journey of salvation by spreading the good news of the Gospel and by comforting those afflicted with pain, illness or demons.

> From that time on, Jesus began to preach and say, "Repent, for the kingdom of heaven is at hand."

> He went around all of Galilee, teaching in their synagogues, proclaiming the gospel of the kingdom, and curing every disease and illness among the people. His fame spread to all of Syria, and **they brought to him all who were sick with various diseases and racked with pain, those who were possessed, lunatics, and paralytics, and he cured them.**
>
> (Matthew 4:17, 23-24)

I find a couple of major thoughts important in this passage. First, the concept that Jesus is the light that was prophesized by Isaiah. Jesus begins his ministry by telling everyone who will listen that the "kingdom of heaven is at hand" – meaning it is here. Jesus is the light, opening the eyes of all who will see, that the Kingdom is in front of them. Matthew connects the words of Isaiah with the first words that Jesus says.

Next, Jesus not only preaches, but he also shows us the way to action right from the very beginning. He does not just preach, he does not just talk, he actually touches people and their lives. It is much easier to talk than to act, but Jesus does not do things that way. He begins, by showing through his own actions that this is how the disciples in his time, and we today, are to minister to all peoples of the world.

In order to cure someone, one must first get close enough to the person to see and hear that they have a problem and care enough about them to do something. That "something" may be easy or extremely difficult. We all have problems, but we also all have the ability to serve others if we just take the time and effort to do so.

Very quickly, people around the region recognized that Jesus cared about people enough to help them. They brought to him their most dire situations. His care and concern for them encouraged them to stop and listen to his greater message of love and hope and eternity.

The Mission of the Disciples

Jesus gave a mission first to the Twelve, and then to Seventy-Two, to preach the Gospel, heal the sick. He described their mission in words that echo the beginning of his own ministry.

> [Jesus] summoned the Twelve and **gave them power and authority over all demons and to cure diseases, and he sent them to proclaim the kingdom of God, and to heal [the sick]. He said to them, "Take nothing for the journey, neither walking stick, nor sack, nor food, nor money, and let no one take a second tunic.** Whatever house you enter stay there and leave from there. And as for those who do not welcome you, when you leave that town, shake the dust from your feet in testimony against them." Then they set out and went from village to village proclaiming the good news and curing diseases everywhere. (Luke 9:1-6)

After the twelve return with news of their journeys, he gathers seventy-two and sends them out. They are to venture out in the same way. Jesus knows that the effort to convert sinners and heal them of their wounds will continue throughout history. He foreshadows our own labors of gathering souls throughout the world and throughout time when he says, "The harvest is abundant but the laborers are few."

> After this the Lord appointed seventy[-two] others whom he sent ahead of him in pairs to every town and place he intended to visit. He said to them, "The harvest is abundant but the laborers are few; so ask the master of the harvest to send out laborers for his harvest. **Go on your way; behold, I am sending you like lambs among wolves. Carry no money bag, no sack, no sandals; and greet no one along the way.** Into whatever house you enter, first

say, 'Peace to this household.' If a peaceful person lives there, your peace will rest on him; but if not, it will return to you. Stay in the same house and eat and drink what is offered to you, for the laborer deserves his payment. Do not move about from one house to another. *Whatever town you enter and they welcome you, eat what is set before you, cure the sick in it and say to them, 'The kingdom of God is at hand for you.'* Whatever town you enter and they do not receive you, go out into the streets and say, 'The dust of your town that clings to our feet, even that we shake off against you.' Yet know this: *the kingdom of God is at hand*. I tell you, it will be more tolerable for Sodom on that day than for that town." (Luke 10:1-12)

As these original disciples of Christ set out on their mission, they must have been a sight to see. They had nothing for the journey, and they would have been walking for days and days to reach out to distant towns. They would have been a dusty, dirty mess by the time they reached another town. We are not told whether or not they were nervous, but we do know that they went, as Christ sent them, bearing the "gifts" of their belief in Jesus, their faith in God, the stories of the "good news" and "power and authority over all demons and to cure diseases."

To me it feels a bit like writing this book. I feel wholly inadequate to the task. I am humbled even to feel called to try to write it, and I struggle with my own frailties to compose it. But I also feel buoyed and shielded by the Holy Spirit. I have no power to save souls, but the words of the Lord have the power to change hearts. Once the words are written, it will be up to the Holy Spirit where they go and to what hearts they may touch.

The words of Our Lord, as carried by the seventy-two are powerful gifts indeed, but let us also think about how they would have been received. Imagine, if today you were approached by people who had been living out in the environment for days or weeks or longer, had no money, one set of clothes, no food, and no apparent means of getting any, and they said to you, "We have met this man that performs miracles and can cure diseases, and he has given us the power to do the same." Would you let them into your house? And, I mean really let them into your house, not just for an afternoon visit or a meal, but to stay for an extended period of time and to provide for all their needs during that time? Or would you shoo away these apparently homeless, crazy men without even looking them in the eye?

It was the opportunity of a lifetime that they offered, actually, the opportunity of eternity. Would you have recognized it? Bigger than buying Apple stock 30 years ago, I wonder if I would recognize the gifts they were bringing? Or, out of fear or discomfort or some even more prejudiced feeling, would I have driven them away? It is a difficult question to face. But driving them away means that this could be the reply: "for those who do not welcome you, when you leave that town, shake the dust from your feet in testimony against them."

To welcome them, I would have had to stop and pay attention long enough to realize that they were people first of all. These were people with an unbounded joy because of their message and their faith. I would need to really listen to the most wonderful, powerful, beloved message in all humanity that can come from the humblest among us.

> They set out and went from village to village proclaiming the good news and curing diseases everywhere.
>
> When the apostles returned, they explained to him what they had done. He took them and withdrew in private. (Luke 9: 6,10)

Like the baby in the manger, or these men on the road, or as we humbly care for a loved one in the middle of the night, it is not about money or fame or shining things, it is about love. I have heard homilies about this passage many times in my life, but as I recall, they have usually focused on Jesus' instructions to the Twelve and less about the people who were meant to be receiving the news from the disciples. Even a footnote in my bible says, "Take nothing for the journey: the absolute detachment required of the disciple leads to complete reliance on God."

The focus, I had come to learn over the years, was on the faith that it must have taken for these men to venture out with nothing but the clothes they were wearing. But now, I believe there is another equally powerful meaning, that of the way the Word of God is received. I am in awe of the fact that so many people to the ends of the earth have listened to this message of love and hope, with no earthly promises, and have accepted it for more than 2,000 years.

Jesus gives the twelve, and all of us, these instructions:

> As you go, make this proclamation: 'The kingdom of heaven is at hand.' Cure the sick, raise the dead, cleanse lepers, drive out demons. Without cost you have received; without cost you are to give. (Matthew 10:7-8)

The message that we are no longer to be governed by earthly worries is not meant just for the disciples. It was for those disciples who listened to the disciples, and those who listened to them, and so on, down to the present day, to us. It is for us to hear – the Kingdom is at hand, right before us.

The Temptation of Jesus

Now compare and contrast the passage of Jesus summoning the disciples and sending them forth with the "good news" to the temptation of Christ by the devil in the desert. When we put these two passages together, we can see the sharp contrast between the promises of God and the promises of the evil one.

> Filled with the holy Spirit, Jesus returned from the Jordan and was led by the Spirit into the desert forty days, to be tempted by the devil. He ate nothing during those days, and when they were over he was hungry. The devil said to him, "If you are the Son of God, command this stone to become bread." Jesus answered him, "It is written, **'One does not live by bread alone.'**" Then he took him up and showed him all the kingdoms of the world in the single instant. The devil said to him, "I shall give to you all this power and their glory; for it has been handed over to me, and I may give it to whoever I wish. All this will be yours, if you worship me." Jesus said to him in reply, "It is written:
>
> > **'You shall worship the Lord, your God, and him alone shall you serve.'"**
>
> Then he led him to Jerusalem, made him stand on the parapet of the temple, and said to him, "If you are the Son of God, throw yourself down from here, for it is written:
>
> > 'He will command his angels concerning you,
> >   to guard you,'
>
> and
>
> > 'with their hands they will support you,
> >   lest you dash your foot against a stone.'"
>
> Jesus said to him in reply, "It also says, **'You shall not put the Lord, your God to the test.'"** When the devil had finished every temptation, he departed from him for a time. (Luke 4: 1-13)

The devil in this passage tempts Jesus with food (bread), power and glory, including all the kingdoms of the world, and protection against all harm, even something as small as stubbing his foot on a stone.

But when Jesus sends out the disciples to preach, they have no food, no extra clothes, no money, no wealth, no glory, no power, nothing to protect them from encountering ills. They only have the Word of God. But that is all that they needed, and all that the people receiving the message needed. That is all we need. God is not trying to tempt us to believe, he is simply telling us the truth. The difference between truth and temptation is the difference between God and the devil.

Bread For His Hunger

Let us take just the first one of these temptations. The devil first tempts Jesus with food. We have all been hungry and we all know that we need food to survive and live. But Jesus answers that, "One does not live on bread alone." In the account from Matthew on the same event, Jesus expands on this thought by saying:

> "One does not live on bread alone,
> but by every word that comes forth from the
> mouth of God." (Matthew 4:4)

It is every such word that can feed us for the life that matters, "eternal life in the ages to come."

To show us that we can rely on him, and that God will also provide for our earthly needs, Jesus performed the Miracle of the Seven Loaves.

> In those days when there again was a great crowd without anything to eat, he summoned the disciples and said, "My heart is moved with pity for the crowd, because they have been with me now for three days and have nothing to eat. If I send them

away hungry to their homes, they will collapse on the way, and some of them have come a great distance." His disciples answered him, "Where can anyone get enough bread to satisfy them here in this deserted place?" Still he asked them, "How many loaves do you have?" "Seven," they replied. He ordered the crowd to sit down on the ground. Then, taking the seven loaves he gave thanks, broke them, and gave them to his disciples to distribute, and they distributed them to the crowd. They also had a few fish. He said the blessing over them and ordered them distributed also. They ate and were satisfied. They picked up the fragments left over—seven baskets. There were about four thousand people. (Mark 8:1-9)

Jesus is concerned and has pity for this large crowd who has been listening to him for three days. The disciples have just a few loaves of bread and a few fish, but they give them up, they offer them up to feed the crowd. Jesus gives thanks to God for the few loaves of bread and fish that they have, but God multiplies what was there until "they ate and were satisfied."

The disciples who were sent out by Jesus were also told not to bring even a second tunic, no extra clothes for the journey. Therefore, all the disciples had to offer was the "word that comes forth from the mouth of God." They are missionaries of the word and we are meant to accept his word, made flesh in the person of Jesus, as the greatest gift that God has ever given the world.

Even so, God understands what we need to live. In Luke, chapter 12, Jesus tells us:

> Therefore I tell you, ***do not worry about your life and what you will eat, or about your body and what you will wear.***

> As for you, do not seek what you are to eat and what you are to drink, and do not worry anymore. All the nations of the world seek for these things, and *your Father knows that you need them. Instead, seek his kingdom, and these other things will be given you besides.* (Luke 12:22, 29-31)

As St. Paul tells the Philippians, in whatever circumstance we find ourselves, God's strength empowers us and provides what we truly need according to His will:

> I [Paul] know indeed how to live in humble circumstances; I know also how to live with abundance. In every circumstance and in all things I have learned the secret of being well fed and of going hungry, of living in abundance and of being in need. I have the strength for everything through him who empowers me. (Philippians 4:12-13)

Power and Glory

Next, the devil tries to tempt Jesus with earthly kingdoms and power and glory. It is clearly a deception because all power and glory already belong to Jesus.

> Jesus approached and said to them, "All power in heaven and on earth has been given to me. Go, therefore, and make disciples of all nations, baptizing them in the name of the Father, and of the Son and of the holy Spirit, teaching them to observe all that I have commanded you. And behold, I am with you always, until the end of the age." (Matthew 28:18-20)

If all power and glory already belong to Jesus, anything we are given in this life also belongs to Jesus, and we are but stewards of what we have been given.

If the devil tempts us with power or glory here on earth, he is nothing more than a conman. "Look here, I have a deed to the Brooklyn Bridge. I will sell it to you for a mere pittance." If you buy that, he will be willing to "sell" you even more; the only price is your eternal soul. The more we chase fame and fortune, the more we are lured by the deceptions of the evil one.

> "Whoever causes one of these little ones who believes in me to sin, it would be better for him to have a great millstone hung around his neck and to be drowned in the depths of the sea. "Woe to the world because of things that cause sin! Such things must come, but woe to the one through whom they come!" (Matthew 18:6-7)

Jesus sends the disciples out with no earthly power or glory. They are walking around with no money and not even a walking stick. They are sent to approach others the same way that God sees us when we approach him. They are a dusty, dirty mess. When we come to God, we come as we are, with our hopes, dreams, ills, sins, struggles and pains. No matter what we do, we cannot dress ourselves up to God, because God already knows who we are in the depth of our hearts and souls.

That is how Jesus commissioned the disciples, they must go as they are. With all their faith and all their failings. They have nothing to share except the word. But, that is enough, because God does not "sell" entrance to the kingdom of Heaven, he wants it to be a *gift* to us. Jesus tells us:

> "Do not be afraid any longer, little flock, for your Father is *pleased to give* you the kingdom." (Luke 12:32)

The ultimate reward of going to Heaven (the kingdom of God) and of being with him forever is the supreme gift from God; we have not earned it – but we can make good use of what we have been given here already. We must understand that we have been created for the good works God intends for us. As the saying goes, "who we are is our gift from God, who we become, is our gift to God."

> For by grace you have been saved through faith, and this is not from you; it is the gift of God; it is not from works, so no one may boast. For we are his handiwork, created in Christ Jesus for the good works that God has prepared in advance, that we should live in them. (Ephesians 2:8-10)

In our lifetimes, God gives us small and large "kingdoms," or "gardens," to manage. He gives each of us our own unique, and special, gifts that we may serve Him and each other. We can do nothing to earn our way or compel our admittance into Heaven. Our gifts are not about us; they are meant for others. We are to serve; we are to love.

We are not created merely for ourselves. If we were, what would be the point? Why have any of us at all?

> Do you not know that your body is a temple of the holy Spirit within you, whom you have from God, and that you are not your own? (1 Corinthians 6:19)

Using our gifts for others is an act of faith. If we truly believe, we affirm who He is and that He wants us to love others, to serve others, by using our gifts for others.

> There are different kinds of spiritual gifts but the same spirit; there are different forms of service but the same Lord; there are different workings but the same God who produces all of them in everyone. To each individual the manifestation of the Spirit *is given for some benefit*. (1 Corinthians 12:4-7)

The benefit is for others, and then as well, for us. Whether we are using our gifts as a teen learning to be responsible, as a parent, den mother, mayor of a town, or Chief Executive Officer of a major corporation, we are all given opportunities to be faithful stewards of what God has given us. These opportunities, and how we manage our own "kingdoms," are ways for us to practice on our own road to eternal life. Are we following Jesus, who is the way, and the truth and the life, or are we following the deceptions of the evil one, who takes us on a path to death, in this life and the next?

> As each one has received a gift, use it to serve one another as good stewards of God's varied grace. (1 Peter: 4:10)

Think of a birthday cake. You are given the gift of the birthday cake by family or friends. It is pure gift, ***but*** it has not been given to you to eat all by yourself. It is not really serving its purpose as a birthday cake until you slice it up and share it with others.

We need to believe and act on the fact that everything we have been given is a gift, on loan from God. We may sometimes think, "I can do anything I want, it's my kingdom or my body, or my household or my company," but that is the temptation of the evil one speaking in your ear.

> "Who, then, is the faithful and prudent servant whom the master will put in charge of his servants to distribute [the] food allowance at the proper time? Blessed is the servant who his master on arrival finds doing so. Truly, I say to you, he will be put in charge of all his property. But if the servant says to himself, '*My master is delayed in coming,' and begins to beat the menservants and the maidservants, to eat and drink and get drunk, then the servant's master will come on an unexpected day and an unknown hour and will punish him severely and assign him a place with the unfaithful*. The servant who knew his master's will but did not make preparations nor act in accord with his will shall be beaten severely;

> and the servant who is ignorant of his master's will but acted in a way deserving of a severe beating shall be beaten only lightly. ***Much will be required of the person entrusted with much, and still more will be demanded of the person entrusted with more.*** " (Luke 12:42-48)

So, if we think that there is no God, or even if we think that there is a 'creator' but he does not care about the workings of man, and we believe we can do anything we want, take anything we want, abuse anyone we want, it is a deception from the evil one. He is leading us on a path of death, in this life and the next.

> Then he said to all, "If anyone wishes to come after me, he must deny himself and take up his cross daily and follow me. For whoever wishes to save his life will lose it, but whoever loses his life for my sake will save it. What profit is there for one to gain the whole world yet lose or forfeit himself? (Luke 9:23-25)

Protection from all Harm

Lastly, the devil tries to tempt Jesus, and us, by a life in which no bad thing will ever happen. Jesus is told by the devil that he can throw himself off the highest point of the temple, and he will come through the ordeal without even a stubbed toe. Since Jesus was fully human, as well as fully God, that certainly would be a reckless thing to do. Jesus' reply is ***"You shall not put the Lord, your God to the test."***

Yes, God is with us always, when good things happen and when bad things happen. God knows every facet of our lives in this world, and he knows that bad things will happen to us. He promises to be with us always, and he loves us so much, that he sent his only Son to save our eternal souls. Many people are familiar with the verse:

> For God so loved the world that he gave his only Son, so that everyone who believes in him might not perish but might have eternal life. (John 3:16)

But the passage continues in a way that shows us that the way to Heaven is the path of light, and the path to eternal death is darkness. Jesus knows that there is sin in the world that causes evil things to happen, but he is here to save us. We have free will; but we cannot continue to "test" God's love by doing evil things and taking the dark path, because the longer we are on that path, the more we condemn ourselves. We cannot do reckless things and expect to come away unscathed.

> For God did not send his son into the world to condemn the world, but that the world might be saved through him. Whoever believes in him will not be condemned, but whoever does not believe has already been condemned, because he has not believed in the name of the only Son of God. And this is the verdict, that the light came into the world, **but people preferred darkness to light, because their works were evil**. For everyone who does wicked things hates the light and does not come toward the light, so that his works might not be exposed. **But whoever lives the truth comes to light, so that his works may be clearly seen as done in God.** (John 3:17-21)

When God sent his Son into the world, he knew, and Jesus knew, that evil would be plotted against him and that he would ultimately be killed through an act of nearly unimaginable evil. Jesus not only accepted the will of the Father, but he went through this ordeal for the love of all of us.

> He [Jesus] said, "The Son of Man must suffer greatly and be rejected by the elders, the chief

priests, and the scribes, and be killed and on the third day be raised." (Luke 9:22)

Jesus did not send the disciples to prevent all bad things from happening to people, but to care for them, to help remove them from the snares of evil, illnesses and demons, to give them comfort, and a pathway to eternal life. They are sent to tell the world that evil has no ultimate power over us when we follow the Lord. As Jesus told his disciples:

> "They will seize and persecute you, they will hand you over to the synagogues and to prisons, and they will have you led before kings and governors because of my name. It will lead to your giving testimony. Remember, you are not to prepare your defense beforehand, for I myself shall give you a wisdom in speaking that all your adversaries will be powerless to resist or refute. You will even be handed over by parents, brothers, relatives, and friends, and they will put some of you to death. You will be hated by all because of my name, ***but not a hair of your head will be destroyed. By your perseverance you will secure your lives.***" (Luke 21:12-19)

Our salvation is eternal, not earthly. Someone may take your life, but your eternal life is in the hands of God. Whenever we carry our cross for God, we are following the path of light to Heaven. We are building a strong foundation to carry us through. Jesus is our strength through trials and anxieties. The devil is continually trying to take our faith and our strength away from us. As Jesus tells us:

> "***Everyone who listens to these words of mine and acts on them*** will be like a wise man who built his house on rock. The rain fell, the floods came, and the winds blew and buffeted the house. But it did not collapse; it had been set solidly on

rock. And everyone who listens to these words of mine but does not act on them will be like a fool who built his house on sand. The rain fell, the floods came, and the winds blew and buffeted the house. And it collapsed and was completely ruined." (Matthew 7:24-27)

We must listen to the words of God and act on them. Again, *"Whoever lives the truth comes to light, so that his works may be clearly seen as done in God." (John 3:21)* By acting on the words of God we are living the truth and moving closer to the light.

Living Water

It is the Word of God that is sufficient for us because your Father knows what you need to ask, or even before you realize it, what you need, and he will give it to you; he does not want us spending all our lives worrying about it. What a wonderful message.

Our focus, then, should be on the kingdom of Heaven, on the living word, the living water. Remember the story of the Samaritan woman at the well who meets Jesus.

> A woman of Samaria came to draw water. Jesus said to her, "Give me a drink." The Samaritan woman said to him, "How can you, a Jew, ask me, a Samaritan woman, for a drink?" (For Jews use nothing in common with Samaritans.) Jesus answered and said to her, "If you knew the gift of God and who is saying to you, 'Give me a drink,' you would have asked him and he would have given you living water." [The woman] said to him, "Sir you do not even have a bucket in the well is deep; where can you get this living water." Jesus answered and said to her, "Everyone who drinks this water will be thirsty again; but whoever drinks the water I shall give will never thirst; the water

> I shall give will become in him a spring of water welling up to eternal life." (John 4:7, 9-11, 13-14)

I have been a Eucharistic Minister for many years. When I am standing with the precious body of Christ or His precious blood, I am privileged to see the eyes and hands and bodies of the people who stand in line to receive. I can often see a reflection of their lives as they approach. I can see the hard work of their hands, the joy, sorrow, or pain in their eyes, and sometimes even the crippling ills of their bodies that have been racked by a lifetime of hard work or cancer or poverty. I try to see them as God must see them, and I am a 'stand-in' for Jesus as he offers his own true body and blood as the most holy of gifts, eternal life.

None of us can claim to be fully worthy of our own accord. This true body and blood of Christ is a pure gift of love and mercy. We can, however, respect the magnificence of this gift and try, with God's help, to present ourselves as worthy and ready as possible.

To respect this gift, I want to be as welcoming to those receiving the precious Body and Blood of Christ, as Jesus himself.

> Then he took the bread, said the blessing, broke it, and gave it to them, saying, "This is my body, which will be given for you; do this in memory of me." And likewise the cup after they had eaten, saying, "This cup is the new covenant in my blood, which will be shed for you. (Luke 22:19-20)

I know first-hand how easily the evil one can get into your mind with thoughts that are not from Christ. As a Eucharistic Minister, I often help to distribute of the Precious Blood when I serve. Not everyone in line receives the Precious Blood, it is not required. I try to offer a welcoming smile to everyone; I even try to make eye contact with those who do not receive, hoping maybe, next time, they will feel welcomed enough to receive.

One day, as I was standing with the Precious Blood of the Eucharist and trying to welcome people to receive, the thought came into my mind, "You are smiling so they will come over to you. You are making this all about you, when it should be about Jesus." All of a sudden, I began to question if this was true. Had I been making it all about myself all these years? As the thought flashed through my mind, the very next man in line said to me, "You have such a welcoming smile."

I was stunned. Never before or after this have I had someone in line say something, anything, to me. It was an immediate answer to an unspoken prayer. It was confirmation that I should continue to try to reach people in my own humble way. The devil may tempt in such subtle ways, but we must always listen to the truth.

The Temptations of Christ and Commission of the Disciples

In Chapter Seven, we will talk about how the sufferings of Christ prefigure all the sufferings we may encounter here in our modern world. Sometimes, it may be difficult to see the very real connection.

The temptations suffered by Christ are like that. These parts of his life show us that he was in fact fully human, they show us why it was so fitting for him to become human. He did it not only to connect the human to the divine in regard to spirituality and eternal love, but also to connect with us in our weaknesses, troubles and failings. And why would he do that? Love.

In our world, what are we told often enough? We are told that we need things of this word; we need hamburgers loaded with an extra patty, or even two, with bacon on top. We are told that reality shows seen by millions can give us fame and importance, even if we may have to be naked or marry someone on first sight. We are told that pharmaceutical drugs can prolong our youth, restore hair or guard us from every type of ailment – until we die.

In stark contrast, what are we told by current disciples, sent out by other disciples, and on and on back to the original disciples – is that there is a Truth. The Word of God is all that we need. The Word can give us joy that is the luxury of luxuries, value in being part of something much bigger than ourselves and protection that lasts forever.

But there will be no guarantee we will not have hard things to endure. Everyone has hard things. Hard things happen to everybody. The disciples might have been cold at night from not having a second tunic. They may have been hungry at times until someone provided them something to eat. They may have suffered ridicule or torture along the way. But with the Word to guide them, the disciples journeyed on and kept their minds on the truth. Truth is a gift from the one who can see past the forest of this human life to eternity. It is the same as what any parent, who can see dangers that a young child cannot, such as a car coming down the street, would want to give.

The Lord gives that to us now for our own journeys. He gives us gifts to use for the benefit of others, to love others and help them love others as well, in an ever-expanding circle that allows all of us to be part of something bigger, for now and for always.

There is another side to all of this. There are the things that are not true. If we learn to want the tastiest foods, notoriety, or money that can give us power over our immediate lives, we draw only into ourselves, instead of being drawn outward toward others. We are drawn to being small, rather than to something larger than just us. We can be told things will be given to us and everything will be easy or that we will have no worries. These things are lies.

The evil one promises these things. Jesus cannot, and did not, promise such things. It would be impossible, therefore, for him to tell us we need to value such things. If he did, he would be like the evil one. He cannot. He cannot give us anything but the truth.

Jesus does not hold us bound to anything. He desires us to be with him forever, but it must be because we choose to seek that. If we do not, if we choose to focus on our own selves, and the things valuable to that focus, we give up the freedom to love as we desire. We are then bound to the things that please our wants or the voices that promise us those things. Jesus did not listen to those voices, although the temptations were put before him. Neither did the disciples when they chose to listen to the voice of Jesus when he told them to go forth with only the truth. Jesus became human to show the disciples, and us, that way.

When we put the Temptations of Christ together with the Commission of the Disciples, we can see a stark difference between God and the devil in our lives. Whereas God tells us the pure truth, the devil needs to lure or tempt us to his side with lies and deceptions.

In Summary:

The Devil Tempts Jesus, and Us:	But, Jesus Sent the Disciples, and Us:	Because Jesus Tells Us:
With bread to satisfy earthly hunger and needs	With no promise of food or money	Eternal life comes from the Bread of Life, that is, the Word of God
With glory, and power over earthly kingdoms	With no promise of earthly power or glory	True glory is to be found in eternal life with God
With protection from all dangers so that no harm will ever come to us	With no promise of a life without trials or hurts	God promises to be with us through all of our trials, and he sends us to do likewise

Psalm 23

Most of us are familiar with Psalm 23. We can choose to read it as simply about our lives here on earth, but it is so much more powerful when we read it as a pathway to endless days with our Lord in Heaven. He is with us always, even when we "walk through the valley of the shadow of death," he will guide us along "right paths" until we are in the "house of the Lord for endless days."

> The LORD is my shepherd;
>   there is nothing I lack.
> In green pastures he makes me lie down;
>   to still waters he leads me;
>   he restores *my soul.*
> **He guides me along *right paths***
>   for the sake of **his name**.
> Even though I walk through the valley of
>   the shadow of death,
>   ***I will fear no evil, for you are with me***;
>   your rod and your staff comfort me.
> You set a table before me
>   in front of my enemies;
> You anoint my head with oil;
>   my cup overflows.
> Indeed, ***goodness and mercy will pursue me***
>   all the days of my life;
> I will dwell in the house of the LORD
>   For *endless days*.

This psalm is about following the right path, the truth, all the way to Heaven. We see God as the good shepherd, guiding us and providing for us and loving us. Even when bad things happen to us or are all around us, with God, there is nothing we shall lack. Ultimately, even if we die by the forces of evil, we will live forever with God.

The Conversion and Ministry of St. Paul

If it is not enough to think of the temptations of Christ, let us look at St. Paul and the ordeal he went through to bring the Gospel to the Gentiles and all the world. How did St. Paul get the courage to leave his old way of life and follow the truth of Christ?

As we recall, St. Paul, who was formerly known as Saul, was converted by a mystical encounter with Christ as he traveled to Damascus to persecute the people who were following "The Way."

> On his journey, as he was nearing Damascus, a light from sky suddenly flashed around him. He fell to the ground and heard a voice saying to him, "Saul, Saul, why are you persecuting me?" He said, "Who are you, sir?" The reply came, "I am Jesus, whom you are persecuting. Now get up and go into the city and you will be told what you must do." The men who were traveling with him stood speechless, for they heard the voice but could see no one. (Acts 9:3-7)

This experience of Christ was so powerful, that Saul eventually became Paul, and he became, arguably, the most fervent messenger of Christianity in all of history. Paul was willing to carry his cross for the Lord. He knew it was the path to Heaven for himself, but also for all with whom he shared his witness.

Paul endured hunger, beatings, vilification, imprisonment and death, all for the sake of the Gospel, because he came to believe it was the truth. Paul knew that whatever bad things happened to him, they were worth the spreading of the Gospel. Just as he does with us, God did not promise Paul a perfect life on earth, but he did promise to stand by him and take him to Heaven.

While Paul was imprisoned, he specifically mentions "a thorn in his flesh," a "messenger of Satan to torment me." While scholars for many years have tried to figure out exactly what he meant, or to whom it referred, the important thing to note is that Paul asks God three times to remove the thorn. God, however, does not remove the thorn from Paul. Instead, God tells him that his "grace is sufficient for you."

> Therefore, that I might not become too elated, a thorn in the flesh was given me, ***an angel of Satan,*** to beat me, to keep me from being too elated. Three times I begged the Lord about this, that it might leave me, but he said to me, "***My grace is sufficient for you,*** for power is made perfect in weakness." I will rather boast most gladly of my weaknesses, in order that ***the power of Christ may dwell with me.*** Therefore, I am content with weaknesses, insults, hardships, persecutions, and constraints, for the sake of Christ; for ***whenever I am weak, then I am strong.*** (2 Corinthians 12:7-10)

It may be all the better for us that we do not to know the details of that "thorn" because we all encounter our own thorns and trials in our lifetimes. God's message stands for all of us equally.

To live "in the flesh," for Paul, meant living with desires such as power or riches or security from all harm above all else. These are the types of things the disciples were specifically not given when they were sent out by Christ. Living with desires and obsessions for such things as these leads to sin. It leads to gluttony, envy of others or greed. That, Paul well knew, meant heading toward death, eternal death. The "wages of sin is death" (Romans 6:23). But God tells him, "my grace is sufficient." Why would God not want to take away the "thorn," the temptation to sin, the temptations that could lead to death?

Paul tells us. "Power is made perfect in weakness." Paul has to learn what that means. The power of God is made perfect in our weakness when we connect ourselves to that power. Whether we currently live in abundance, or whether we lack even certain basics of life, God is always with us to protect our souls.

When we rely totally on Christ, when we understand that God has not promised us power or riches or security from all harm, when we rely on him to resist temptations, or when we willingly carry the burdens that we have been given in our lives, we are telling him we truly believe, without any holding back. We tell him, with our deepest honesty, that we know he is near and that he cares. When we connect ourselves to him, we connect our weakness to his perfection. We prepare ourselves to connect with him in the life after this. That is why Paul can "boast."

The Psalmist we quoted has similar feelings. When he relies on the Lord alone, he can say, "there is nothing I shall lack." The Psalmist can walk through a "valley of the shadow of death," where shadowy figures of the devil tempt him with sin and eternal death, but if he follows the "right path," if he lives "for the sake of his name," he can "dwell in the house of the Lord for endless days."

In our lives, we will be tormented by temptations or an array of troubles, but God will be with us through them all. If we bear our torments, weaknesses and troubles for the sake of Christ, our weaknesses will be our strength as well.

The Good Samaritan

Many of us are familiar with the story of the Good Samaritan, and its message about how to treat others with mercy, regardless of who they are, or what their outward appearance or circumstances may be. The story is taught to even the youngest of children because the message is plain.

> There was a scholar of the law who stood up to test [Jesus] and said, "*Teacher, what must I do to inherit eternal life?*" *Jesus said to him, "What is written in the law? How do you read it?*" He said in reply, "You shall love the Lord, your God with all your heart, with all your being, with all your

strength, and with all your mind, and your neighbor as yourself." He replied to him, "You have answered correctly; do this and you will live."

But because he wished to justify himself, he said to Jesus, "And who is my neighbor?" Jesus replied, "A man fell victim to robbers as he went down from Jerusalem to Jericho. They stripped and beat him and went off leaving him half-dead. A priest happened to be going down that road, but when he saw him, he passed on the opposite side. Likewise a Levite came to the place, and when he saw him, he passed by on the opposite side. But a Samaritan traveler who came upon him was moved with compassion at the sight. He approached the victim, poured oil and wine over his wounds and bandaged them. Then he lifted him up on his own animal, took him to an inn, and cared for him. The next day he took out two silver coins and gave them to the innkeeper with the instruction, 'Take care of him. If you spend more than what I have given you, I shall repay you on the way back.' Which of these three, in your opinion, was neighbor to the robbers' victim?" He answered, "The one who treated him with mercy." Jesus said to him "Go and do likewise."

(Luke 10:25-37)

Now, let us focus on the first part of the story. When the scholar of the law asks Jesus about the path to eternal life, Jesus answers. "What is written in the law? How do you read it?" He clearly points the man to the Law of Moses given by God, and says, "Do this and you shall live."

As I have been exploring the question about choosing Heaven or Hell, I am noticing more and more that Jesus did not come with entirely new laws, but he came more with extensions of and explanations about how to live out the laws of God. He came from our Father, to teach us the wisdom of the laws that God had already laid out for us. We, as people, and by this I mean all peoples everywhere, did not, and do not, really understand the laws that God laid out for us. We are much like children who are taught to say "please" and "thank you," or our ABCs by rote, but it is only later in life that we begin to understand the true meaning of what we have been taught.

When the scholar of the law, someone who we surmise, by virtue of his title, should understand the commandments of God, replies, "You shall love the Lord, your God with all your heart, with all your being, with all your strength, and with all your mind, and your neighbor as yourself." Jesus tells him that he has answered correctly.

Yet, next in the story, we find out, the scholar wishes to justify himself and thereby demonstrates that he does not fully understand the commandments, or even the meaning of his answer to Jesus, at all. He can recite the law, but the true answer is not in his heart. When he asks, "Who is my neighbor?," we learn that his comprehension is only about as deep as the children just learning their ABCs. He has learned only the "do's and do nots" of the Ten Commandments, not how we are to use the commandments to love one another.

Jesus tells this story to explain that "neighbor" has been used by God to describe "everybody" and "anybody." The victim on the side of the road and the Samaritan can be any man or every man. So, when Jesus says, "This I command you; love one another" (John 15:17), Jesus means that we should truly love one another, and not just go through the motions of the original commandments given to us by God. He says this after he has washed the feet of the disciples at the Last Supper. He speaks the words after he had done the act.

When we truly love one another, we can wash each other of anything that keeps us apart. It may be dirt from the road, or it may be illness, or it may be sin, or it may be other hurts. True love sees past these things. True love hugs the person with leprosy or HIV, as Princess Diana did, true love picks up the child off the street in India, as Mother Teresa did, and true love forgives our family members or friends with whom we have perhaps not been speaking for years.

Jesus explains, "*I give you a new commandment: love one another. As I have loved you, so you also should love one another.*" (John 13:34). This is totally consistent with the commandments we have already been given. It is the fulfillment of how we are to live out the commandments. It is an explanation of how to put the commandments into our hearts. It is not about the "do nots" of murder or envy or theft, but about seeing others as God sees us – even through the dirt, and illness, and sin of our lives.

In his letter to the Romans, St. Paul tells us:

> Owe nothing to anyone, except to love one another; *for the one who loves another has fulfilled the law. The commandments,* "You shall not commit adultery; you shall not kill; you shall not steal; you shall not covet," and whatever other commandment there may be, *are summed up in this saying, [namely] "You shall love your neighbor as yourself."* Love does no evil to the neighbor; hence, love is the fulfillment of the law. (Romans 13:8-10)

St. Paul specifically tells us that all of God's commandments are "summed up in this saying, 'You shall love your neighbor as yourself.'" In saying this, he is still pointing us back to the original commandments. We are still meant to observe the commandments given by God to Moses.

In the Gospel of Matthew, Jesus explains that, to truly love one another, we must become the servant of those we love. Love is about sacrifice. This passage is also a denunciation of how the Pharisees give us the rules but do not follow them. He tells us that their "do as I say, not as I do" attitude will ultimately result in their being brought low.

> Then Jesus spoke to the crowds and to his disciples, saying, "The scribes and the Pharisees have taken their seat on the chair of Moses. Therefore, ***do and observe all things whatsoever they tell you, but do not follow their example***. For they preach but they do not practice. They tie up heavy burdens [hard to carry] and lay them on people's shoulders, but they will not lift a finger to move them. All their works are performed to be seen. ***The greatest among you must be your servant***. Whoever exalts himself will be humbled; but whoever humbles himself will be exalted." (Matthew 23:1-5, 11-12)

When I read this passage, the word "all" stood out for me. "Do and observe *all* things whatsoever they tell you" that come from the "chair of Moses." The commandments that come from Moses are a gift from God, a guidance on the path to Heaven. Jesus tells us that they have a truth in them that is not a reflection of how the scribes and Pharisees behave. We must respect the Pharisees to the extent that they have the "word of God" to share with us, but we must also recognize the hypocrisy of their actions. He helps us to discern the difference and gives us a path of reason.

We face the same kinds of hypocrisy today. We find politicians, business leaders and media executives, and film/television stars who profess disdain for certain behaviors, only to find out that they are guilty of those exact behaviors. People end up choosing Hell when they follow their own selfish paths rather than listening to the words of the Father. It is a slippery slope.

While we are meant to use reason to discern the difference, Jesus also tells us that we are not meant to judge others. Judging implies condemning. Again, love, the ultimate commandment, is about giving of oneself to others. As Jesus told his disciples"

> "Stop judging and you will not be judged. Stop condemning and you will not be condemned. Forgive and you will be forgiven. Give and gifts will be given to you; a good measure, packed together, shaken down, and overflowing, will be poured into your lap. For the measure with which you measure will in return be measured out to you." (Luke 6:37-38)

The Canaanite Woman

You may recall the story of the Canaanite woman who had a daughter who was very ill. She approached Jesus and begged him for help. At that time, Jews and Canaanites would not have anything to do with one another, so her request to Jesus would have been a scandal for both the Jews as well as her family and friends.

> [Then Jesus] withdrew to the region of Tyre and Sidon. And behold, a Canaanite woman of that district came and called out, "Have pity on me, Lord, Son of David! My daughter is tormented by a demon." But he did not say a word in answer to her. His disciples came and asked him, "Send her away, for she keeps calling out after us." He said in reply, "I was sent only to the lost sheep of the house of Israel." But the woman came and did him homage, saying, "Lord, help me." He said in reply, "It is not right to take the food of the children and throw it to the dogs." She said, "Please, Lord, for even the dogs eat the scraps that fall from the table of their masters." Then Jesus said to her in reply, "O woman, great is your faith! Let it be done for you as you wish." And her daughter was healed from that hour. (Matthew 15:21-28)

This is a story that many people find troubling. Why would Jesus say, "It is not right to take the food of the children and throw it to the dogs?" It is difficult to think of a kind and gentle Jesus even uttering these kinds of words. Is he really comparing this woman with a sick child to a dog?

But along with the great faith of the woman, it is the "judgment" of the disciples that jumps out of this story to me.

Jesus is presented with a woman asking for help. He also has his disciples around him, and he understood what they were thinking. So, he walks silently along as if ignoring the woman, waiting for who will act next. It is the disciples who are irritated by the woman and ask Jesus to "send her away, for she keeps calling after us."

Then, Jesus says what is really on the minds of the disciples, "I was sent only to the lost sheep of the house of Israel." The disciples now feel justified themselves.

The disciples have previously seen and have been in awe of the wonderful healings that Jesus has performed. They have witnessed his love and compassion and pity for so many others; so why would they not want him to help her? The answer is that she is obviously not a Jew, so they must believe she does not deserve his help. Had they learned nothing from following Jesus along the way?

When Jesus says, "it is not right to take the food of the children and throw it to the dogs," he is still reflecting *their* judgment, *their* disdain for this woman. According to the disciples in the story, they, and the Jews, are the worthy children. Everyone else is the equivalent of a dog. They are self-righteous; they are thinking, "we are special," everyone else is unworthy. Somewhere along the way, they have replaced Jesus' messages and acts of love with their own judgments. They have taken a wrong path and stopped listening to Jesus' voice.

How many times have we judged someone as being unworthy of Jesus' love? How many times have we made that judgment based upon race or gender or clothes or perceived sin or something else? We forget, in that moment, that God loves us all.

> "For he makes his sun rise on the bad and the good,
> and causes rain to fall on the just and the unjust."
> (Matthew 5:45)

It is not, however, a matter of being worthy of God's love. None of us is "worthy" of God's love. The woman understands that she is unworthy of God's love. Yet, she persists and begs for pity. She is asking for a gift. God's love is a gift; it is mercy given freely to ***all*** of us, to ***each*** of us.

Even though she knows that she is not worthy, when she says, "Please, Lord, for even the dogs eat the scraps that fall from the table of their masters," she is saying that even the smallest gift of God, even a scrap of pity that falls from his table, is worth risking everything. She is literally risking everything in her life, her standing in her community, and perhaps even her livelihood, for speaking with a man, especially for speaking with a Jew.

Jesus recognized her faith the first moment she cried out to him as "Lord." He also recognized the disdain of the disciples. Jesus sees all of us for what we are, for what we think and what we believe. He knows all of us as intimately as a mother or father know what their mischievous children are up to, and he loves us all with unequalled compassion.

It is that unequalled compassion, not just for some, but for all, that is the reason why he says to the woman, "O woman, great is your faith! Let it be done for you as you wish." It is a matter of faith. All who believe in him and follow his way can receive his gifts. In healing the woman's daughter, he is not only telling this to her, but, just as importantly, he is doing this as a matter of instruction to his disciples. They are the ones whom he will ultimately be sending out without food, or clothes or money, to take his word to all who will hear, not only to the Jewish people, but to the whole world. If they are going to be able to tell others about him properly, it is they who must understand the truth of who he is and why he came.

It is hard for us to sometimes comprehend how the disciples did not understand Jesus or his messages. We can think of them as larger than life, chosen men of Christ. It is easier to apply negative judgments to the scribes and Pharisees whom we hear about in other stories of the Gospels. They are easier to dismiss because they obviously did not understand the true meaning of the law or Jesus. They looked for any opportunity to dismiss Jesus' teachings and validate their own interpretations of the law. How often do we do the same?

While it may be easier to see fault in the scribes and Pharisees, and less easy to see it in the disciples, it is all that much harder to turn the mirror of prejudice on ourselves. How many times do we see ourselves as worthy, then consciously, or unconsciously, judge another to be unworthy because they are not Catholic or Evangelical, or White or Black, or "pure" by some other fabricated standard? How often do we dismiss someone as unworthy because *we* view them as homeless or addicted to drugs or an illegal alien or some other category? Jesus wants us to stop making judgements like that. Period.

While we need to stop judging others, we also need to understand our own unworthiness before God. The woman understands she is unworthy but begs for a gift of grace from God's love – the removal of a "demon" from her daughter.

What are the "demons" in the lives of our children? What are the "demons" in our own lives? Drug abuse? Hatred of others? Lust? Pornography? Divorce? Abortion? Abusive or corrosive relationships? Bitterness? Blame?

We can remove these demons from our lives if we, like the woman, cry out to Jesus. "Have pity on me, Lord, Son of David!" We must not be afraid. We must not be afraid to ask. We must rely on the mercy and grace and love of God, our Father.

I have come to understand that this is one of the messages of the Adoration event. God wants us to pray to him with all our heart. When I was pleading with Jesus to save one soul, ten souls, a million souls, a billion souls, it was not disrespectful! It was how God wants us to pray – with abandon.

We are all just as worthy or unworthy as this woman. But, God loves us. We can ask for anything! We need to ask from the depths of our soul. Because nothing, ***no thing***, is impossible for God!

We also must teach our children the faith. We must teach them how to pray. We must teach them, so that Jesus may save them.

> And we have this confidence in him, that if we ask anything according to his will, he hears us. And if we know that he hears us in regard to whatever we ask, we know that what we have asked him for is ours. If anyone sees his brother sinning, if the sin is not deadly, he should pray to God and he will give him life. This is only for those whose sin is not deadly. There is such a thing as deadly sin, about which I do not say that you should pray. All wrongdoing is sin, but there is sin that is not deadly.
>
> We know that no one begotten by God sins; but the one begotten by God he protects, and the evil one cannot touch him. We know that we belong to God, and the whole world is under the power of the evil one. We also know that the Son of God has come and has given us discernment to know the one who is true. And we are in the one who is true, in his Son Jesus Christ. He is the true

> God and eternal life. Children, be on your guard against idols.
>
> (1 John 5:14-21)

It is our duty as children of God to discern what is right and true and to follow the voice of our Savior, Jesus Christ. When we do not, we are training ourselves to listen to the voice of the evil one in the world.

God is Limitless

When we pray, our prayers must be from the heart and limitless, because God is limitless. It is only our fears and our limited human minds that constrain our prayers. As the angel tells Mary during his annunciation of the birth of Jesus: "For nothing will be impossible for God." (Luke 1:37)

In Isaiah, we find a passage that not only describes God's desire to hear and answer our unbridled prayers, but also reveals the limits of our imagination and the lack of faith we have in our prayers.

> Again the LORD spoke to Ahaz: Ask for a sign from the LORD, your God; let it be deep as Sheol, or high as the sky! But Ahaz answered, "I will not ask! I will not tempt the Lord!" Then he said: Listen, house of David! Is it not enough that you weary human beings? Must you also weary my God? Therefore the Lord himself will give you a sign; the young woman, pregnant and about to bear a son, shall name him Emmanuel. (Isaiah 7:10-14)

The Lord wants us to ask for the biggest, most precious desires of our hearts, but we often turn away and refuse to ask out of fear or our perceived limitations. As in the passage above, the Jews had been praying for a Messiah to save them. When Ahaz refuses to ask, even after being told to ask, God returns with a gift that is beyond his imagination. God announces he will send the gift of a

Messiah to save, not only the Jews, but all of humankind!

> Now this is how the birth of Jesus Christ came about. When his mother Mary was betrothed to Joseph, but before they lived together, she was found with child through the holy Spirit. Joseph her husband, since he was a righteous man, yet unwilling to expose her to shame, decided to divorce her quietly. Such was his intention when, behold, the angel of the Lord appeared to him in a dream and said, "Joseph, son of David, do not be afraid to take Mary your wife into your home. *For it is through the holy Spirit that this child has been conceived in her. She will bear a son and you are to name him Jesus, because he will save his people from their sins."* All this took place to fulfill what the Lord had said through the prophet:
>
> *"Behold, the virgin shall be with child
> and bear a son,
> and they shall name him Emmanuel,"*
>
> *which means "God is with us."* When Joseph awoke, he did as the angel of the Lord had commanded him and took his wife into his home. (Matthew 1:18-24)

The Jews could not conceive of a Messiah that would save all people. They could not imagine that a divine plan to save "*his people*" would mean that *all* people would be saved.

During the Adoration event, when I was witness to a soul walking away from Jesus at the moment of death, I wanted, more than anything I could have previously imagined in my life, for Jesus to save that soul from Hell. I screamed over and over to the soul in my head, "Don't choose Hell, don't choose Hell! Look at His eyes! Look at His Love!" Then I screamed to Jesus, "Don't let him choose hell, don't let him choose Hell! Look one more time!" It was such a desperate cry. It was as if I felt the pain of a mother watching her son or daughter stepping off a great cliff into a black crevasse with no way back and I was pleading to stop him/her before the fall.

Then I found myself pleading for the salvation of many more souls. It was a plea from the farthest depths of my soul, almost cried out as a demand. "Save one soul, save ten souls, save a million souls, a billion souls." I cried out this prayer over and over again in my mind, more times than I could count.

When the event was over, I first thought that this prayer was beyond audacious and disrespectful. How could I, a mere unworthy human, scream this way to our Lord? Inside me, I always knew that it had been the right thing to do, that it was how I was meant to pray, but there was also this little gnat inside me whispering that it was wrong.

It was during one of these moments of doubt that I found the passage from Isaiah about Ahaz:

> Again the LORD spoke to Ahaz: ***Ask for a sign from the LORD, your God; let it be deep as Sheol, or high as the sky***! (Isaiah 7:10)

It was the Lord who told Ahaz to ask for a sign from God. Let it be deep as Sheol, (which is a Hebrew word meaning the "underworld" or abode of the dead), or as high as the sky!

Then it became so clear to me. ***This*** is how the Lord wants us to pray! He wants us to pray for things as large and deep as anything we can imagine! He wants us to pray with absolute abandon! He wants us to pray for ***all*** souls. For nothing - ***no thing*** - is impossible for God!

This is the prayer for the salvation of souls that I have been praying for all my life in the verses of Away in a Manger:

> *Be near me Lord, Jesus. I ask thee to stay,*
> *close by me forever and love me, I pray.*
>
> *Bless all the dear children in thy tender care,*
> *and take us to Heaven to live with thee there!*

I feel the love of Jesus so deeply in my heart that it is overwhelming. I cry every time I hear even the first few notes of the song. *Every* time!

It is like the Chaplet (see Chapter Nine), formed of the Fatima Prayer, that was taught to me by Our Blessed Mother to take our prayers directly to her son.

> *Oh, my Jesus, forgive us our sins.*
> *Save us from the fires of Hell.*
> *Lead all souls to Heaven,*
> *Especially those in most need of thy mercy.*
>
> *Amen.*

That is what God wants us to ask for – the salvation of all souls! Every soul. Especially those in most need of God's mercy. Who could possibly be in more need of God's mercy than a soul turning away from Jesus and choosing Hell!

So, it is not disrespectful at all to pray for the salvation of a billion souls. It is right. It is pure. It still is less than what God can conceive. And, while we cannot imagine how big that is, He sent us his only Son for the salvation of *every* soul!

CHAPTER FIVE
Why Choose Heaven?

I rejoiced when they said to me,
"Let us go to the house of the LORD." (Psalm 122:1)

To many people, the question, "Why choose Heaven?" may sound just as strange as the question, "Why would anyone choose Hell?"

The direct answer is that we must choose. One way or the other. One path or the other. Every day with every decision, we are making a choice for Heaven or Hell. Where do you want to spend eternity?

If we have strayed from the path to Heaven, we can always change our direction along the way. God will always take us back. He is with us always, but he has given us free will to make our own choices, and he will not make them for us, just as he gives it to our own children and we cannot make their life choices for them.

But we must begin to fully know within our hearts, that when we choose Heaven, when we choose Jesus, He will make us a new creation:

> ***So whoever is in Christ is a new creation: the old things have passed away; behold, new things have come.*** (2 Corinthians 5:17)

The Greatest Commandment

We choose Heaven to fulfill the first and greatest commandment. The first commandment is to love the Lord your God with all your heart and mind and soul.

> Whoever is without love does not know God, for ***God is love.*** (1 John 4:8)

God is love. Therefore, it is Love that created us. He made us to love him and to be with him for all eternity. The way we show

God our love is not only through how we praise him, but also through how we love one another. When we love someone, we want to be with them.

> One thing I ask of the LORD;
>   this I seek:
> To dwell in the LORD's house
>   all the days of my life,
> To gaze on the LORD's beauty,
>   to visit his temple.
> (Psalm 27:4)

It is because we are meant to live forever with God that explains why the Psalmist is seeking to find his way there. In the end, there really is only one thing we can seek from God, to be with him always.

Everything – every thing – is about love. Love is both the why and how we choose Heaven.

The Two Greatest Commandments

A Pharisee tries to trip up Jesus with his question about the greatest of commandments, Jesus instead answers him plainly and explains even more:

> "Teacher, which commandment in the law is the greatest?" He said to him, "You shall love the Lord, your God, with all your heart, with all your soul, and with all your mind. This is the greatest and the first commandment. The second is like it: You shall love your neighbor as yourself. The whole law and the prophets depend on these two commandments." (Matthew 22:36-40)

The whole law and the prophets depend on these two commandments. The whole law – all of it – in it love is everything. Without love, we can not know God.

How can love be everything? Because with love there is joy and blessings and abundance and closeness. When we love, we are preparing our souls for eternity with God. When we show love, we help others prepare their souls for eternity with God. By showing love to others, we give them a tiny glimpse of how it feels to be loved by God and for God.

Without love there is bitterness and hatred and deception and jealousy and separation from God and others. When we choose to be without love, we choose separation. It is the choice of our souls for Hell, either on this earth or for eternity.

The Parable of the Judgment of the Nations

The Parable of the Judgment of the Nations is another story with which many of us are familiar. In the story, at the end of times, the Son of Man separates the sheep from the goats. The sheep represent those going to eternal glory in Heaven and the goats represent those going to eternal punishment and torture. The parable is found in Matthew, Chapter 25. It begins as Jesus says to his disciples:

> "When the Son of Man comes in his glory, and all the angels with him, he will sit upon his glorious throne, and all the nations will be assembled before him. And he will separate them one from another, as a shepherd separates the sheep from the goats. He will place the sheep on his right and the goats on his left. Then the king will say to those on his right, '*Come, you who are blessed by my Father. Inherit the kingdom prepared for you from the foundation of the world.*'" (Matthew 25: 31-34)

Jesus welcomes the lambs who have been saved. They are blessed by God and will inherit the "kingdom prepared for [them] from the foundation of the world." God has been preparing *your* soul for Heaven from the beginning of time – since the foundation of the world. What a glorious image, that God has loved your very soul since forever and for forever.

In the parable, Jesus then goes on to explain how we attain what God has prepared for our souls:

> "For I was hungry and you gave me food, I was thirsty and you gave me drink, a stranger and you welcomed me, naked and you clothed me, ill and you cared for me, in prison and you visited me.' Then the righteous will answer him and say, 'Lord, when did we see you hungry and feed you, or thirsty and give you drink? When did we see you a stranger and welcome you, or naked and clothe you? When did we see you ill or in prison, and visit you?' And the king will say to them in reply, 'Amen, I say to you, whatever you did for one of these least brothers of mine, you did for me.'"
> (Matthew 25:35-40)

We attain our true place with God by seeing, and loving, God in others. This is the fulfillment of both the first and second of the greatest commandments. First, love God. Then, love one another. Because "whatever you did for one of these least brothers of mine, you did for me." If we truly and faithfully do one, we naturally do the other.

However, we can break the first commandment when we break the second. The two commandments go hand in hand, we cannot say that we truly and faithfully love God if we do not love each other.

> "Then he will say to those on his left, 'Depart from me, you accursed, into the eternal fire prepared for the devil and his angels. For I was hungry and you gave me no food, I was thirsty and you gave me no drink, a stranger and you gave me no welcome, naked and you gave me no clothing, ill and

> in prison, and you did not care for me.' Then they will answer and say, 'Lord, when did we see you hungry or thirsty or a stranger or naked or ill or in prison, and not minister to your needs?' He will answer them, 'Amen, I say to you, what you did not do for one of these least ones, you did not do for me.'" (Matthew 25:41-45)

At its core, all our life is about the destination of our eternal souls. The choices we make, and how we treat one another every day lead us along a path directed toward Heaven or Hell. In the final line of the parable, the message is clear that our earthly choices set us on one path or another:

> "And these will go off to eternal punishment, but the righteous to eternal life." (Matthew 25:46)

God gives us these lessons because he loves us. He wants to make it clear to us the reality of the consequences of the choices we make. This is the word of God that has been planted in your heart and in your soul.

> ***Humbly welcome the word that has been planted in you and is able to save your souls.*** (James 1:21)

We must choose. We must make a choice between Heaven and Hell. We cannot stand idly by and expect that the right things will happen. If we do not consciously choose the path toward Heaven, we can easily be deceived onto the path toward Hell.

We must follow the light because there is deception and evil hidden in the darkness.

> No one has ever seen God. Yet, if we love one another, God remains in us, and his love is brought to perfection in us. (1 John 4:12)

It is the truth. God cannot lie.

> Blessed is the man who does not walk
>> in the counsel of the wicked,
> Nor stand in the way of sinners,
>> nor sit in company with scoffers.
> Rather, the law of the LORD is his joy;
>> and on his law he meditates day and night.
> He is like a tree
>> planted near streams of water,
>> that yields its fruit in season;
> Its leaves never wither;
>> whatever he does prospers.
> (Psalm 1:1-3)

"He is like a tree planted near streams of water, that yields its fruit in season." In many ways this is how I feel about writing this book. I keep telling people that the book is "pouring out of me," or "flowing out of me." These are the "streams of water," and they are producing the "fruit" of this book in due season. The words are taking their time to ripen.

> You anoint my head with oil;
>> my cup overflows.
> (Psalm 23:5)

For years now, I have been clipping and saving Bible verses. These verses are ones that jump out at me and stop me in my tracks, so to speak, when I read them. Many of these are the words of scripture that have found their way into the book. These are God's words. They are meant for us to find them and to provide our pathway to Heaven.

I liken these scripture passages to Easter Eggs, and I am on a grand Easter Egg hunt. Each little passage is like finding a treasure that is really meant to be found, not hidden. They are in the tall grass or behind the leg of a chair, just nestled enough to still be in plain view.

We are all on this Easter Egg hunt. The words of scripture are colorful and living and vibrant; they are so easy to find that they glow with the happiness of doing God's will. But, we must search for them; seek them. When we find them, we must reach out and grab them.

They are "pearls of wisdom" or the "empty tomb" that is really the resurrected Christ. They lead us to God, our Heavenly Father. He wants us to be with him in Heaven forever. That is why he sent us his ultimate Easter gift in the breaking of the bonds of sin and death through the resurrection of his Son, Jesus.

> Indeed, the word of God is living and effective, sharper than any two-edged sword, penetrating even between soul and spirit, joints and marrow, and able to discern reflections and thoughts of the heart. (Hebrews 4:12)

The words of God *are living*, even today. When I read a passage of the Bible or you read a passage, it may have a different meaning for you than for me. The words may even strike you differently on different days. God uses these words to stir our hearts and our desire to be with him always. The words written in this little book are not meant to replace your own discoveries in reading the Bible, or when attending Mass, but maybe to nudge you back toward them and to help you find and reach out for your own Easter Eggs full of love and joy.

Discerning the Word of God

You must discern your own path toward God. Test everything. Do not listen to the counsel of the wicked or the sinners or the scoffers. Test my words. I have no authority for writing them. As John says:

> Beloved, do not trust every spirit but test the spirits to see whether they belong to God, be-

> cause many false prophets have gone out into the world. This is how you can know the Spirit of God: every spirit that acknowledges Jesus Christ come in the flesh belongs to God, and every spirit that does not acknowledge Jesus does not belong to God. This is the spirit of the antichrist that, as you heard, is to come, but in fact is already in the world. You belong to God, children, and you have conquered them, for the one who is in you is greater than the one who is in the world. They belong to the world; accordingly, their teaching belongs to the world, and the world listens to them. We belong to God, and anyone who knows God listens to us, while anyone who does not belong to God refuses to hear us. This is how we know the spirit of truth and the spirit of deceit. (1 John 4:1-6)

John continues in this passage to explain the everlasting and faithful love that God has for us. God is love. What more could God do for us than to send us his Son and send us his Spirit. For me, this is the 'why' to choose Heaven – to be close to this love forever.

> Beloved, let us love one another, because love is of God; everyone who loves is begotten by God and knows God. Whoever is without love does not know God, for God is love. In this way the love of God was revealed to us: God sent his only Son into the world so that we might have life through him. In this is love: not that we have loved God, but that he loved us and sent his Son as expiation for our sins. ***Beloved, if God so loved us, we also must love one another***. No one has ever seen God. Yet, if we love one another, God remains in us, and his love is brought to perfection in us.

This is how we know that we remain in him and he in us, that he has given us of his Spirit. Moreover, we have seen and testify that the Father sent his Son as savior of the world. *Whoever acknowledges that Jesus is the Son of God, God remains in him and he in God. We have come to know and to believe in the love God has for us.*

(1 John 4:7-16)

Testing Ourselves and Our Choices

How do we hold the mirror up to our own choices?

> I command you: be strong and steadfast! Do not fear nor be dismayed, for the LORD, your God, is with you wherever you go. (Joshua 1:9)

God, through Moses, gave all of us the pathway for living a good life here on earth, and therefore, the pathway to Heaven when he gave us his commandments. As our Father, God wants only good things for his children. Moses said to the people:

> *Hear the statutes and ordinances I am teaching you to observe, that you may live*, and may enter in and take possession of the land which the LORD, the God of your ancestors, is giving you. In your observance of the commandments of the LORD, your God, which I am commanding you, you shall not add to what I command you nor subtract from it… Observe them carefully, for this is your wisdom and discernment in the sight of the peoples, who will hear of all these statutes and say, "This great nation is truly a wise and discerning people." For what great nation is there that has gods so close to it as the LORD, our God, is to us whenever we call upon him? Or what great nation has statutes and

> ordinances that are as just as this whole law which I am setting before you today?
>
> However, be on your guard and be very careful not to forget the things your own eyes have seen, nor let them slip from your heart as long as you live, but make them known to your children and to your children's children."
>
> (Deuteronomy 4:1-2, 6-9)

How can we teach our children and our children's children what we do not know ourselves? Can we truly say that we love God with our whole heart, our whole soul and our whole mind if we do not study his words and follow them? Really?

Training Ourselves to Hear God's Voice and See the Light

There are many bible stories that help us to understand that we must follow the light to Heaven, not the darkness to Hell.

We must train ourselves to study the word of God. We must spend time with him in prayer. It is only through these steps that we will hear His voice and see His light.

> My sheep hear my voice; I know them, and they follow me. (John 10:27)

In the story of the birth of Jesus, the Magi, or Three Kings, follow a star to Bethlehem. We do not know much about the Magi from the story, but since they had noticed the "star at its rising" we can assume that they studied the stars and that they had traveled a great distance from the east.

> When Jesus was born in Bethlehem of Judea, in the days of King Herod, behold, magi from the east arrived in Jerusalem, saying, "Where is the

newborn king of the Jews? We saw his star at its rising and have come to do him homage." When King Herod heard this, he was greatly troubled, and all Jerusalem with him. Assembling all the chief priests and the scribes of the people, he inquired of them where the Messiah was to be born. They said to him, "In Bethlehem of Judea, for thus it has been written through the prophet:

> 'And you, Bethlehem, land of Judah,
> are by no means least among the
>   rulers of Judah;
> since from you shall come a ruler,
> who is to shepherd my people Israel.'"

Then Herod called the magi secretly and ascertained from them the time of the star's appearance. He sent them to Bethlehem and said, "Go and search diligently for the child. When you have found him, bring me word, that I too may go and do him homage." After their audience with the king they set out. And behold, the star that they had seen at its rising preceded them, until it came and stopped over the place where the child was. They were overjoyed at seeing the star, and on entering the house they saw the child with Mary his mother. They prostrated themselves and did him homage. Then they opened their treasures and offered him gifts of gold, frankincense, and myrrh. And having been warned in a dream not to return to Herod, they departed for their country by another way. (Matthew 2:1-12)

The Magi had studied the workings of God in nature, and trained themselves to notice the signs. They trusted and believed enough of what they saw that they chose to disrupt their lives and take a very long journey. They were rewarded in their pursuit. They were "overjoyed at seeing the star, and on entering the house they saw the child with Mary his mother."

Like the soul during the Adoration Event, if we but turn around and see the light, we will find Jesus and Mary, his mother, fighting for our eternal souls.

The Parable of the Ten Virgins

Jesus told the Parable of the Ten Virgins to explain to us that we must persevere in keeping the light of God in our lives always.

> [Jesus said to them:] "Then the kingdom of heaven will be like ten virgins who took their lamps and went out to meet the bridegroom. Five of them were foolish and five were wise. The foolish ones, when taking their lamps, brought no oil with them, but the wise brought flasks of oil with their lamps. Since the bridegroom was long delayed, they all became drowsy and fell asleep. At midnight, there was a cry, 'Behold, the bridegroom! Come out to meet him!' Then all those virgins got up and trimmed their lamps. The foolish ones said to the wise, 'Give us some of your oil, for our lamps are going out.' But the wise ones replied, 'No, for there may not be enough for us and you. Go instead to the merchants and buy some for yourselves.' While they went off to buy it, the bridegroom came and those who were ready went into the wedding feast with him. Then the door was locked. Afterwards the other virgins came and said, 'Lord, Lord, open the door for us!' But he said in reply, 'Amen, I say to you, I do not know you.' Therefore, stay awake, for you know neither the day nor the hour." (Matthew 25:1-13)

Like the seed that fell among the rocks in the Parable of the Sower, the five foolish virgins started out on the right path at the beginning of the story; they had light. Their light burned strong, but it was used up quickly.

All ten virgins start out on the road, or path, of the bridegroom. The bridegroom is on the road, or path, to the wedding party, which is Heaven.

The choices of the foolish virgins have left them without enough light to get them to the wedding feast. The decisions that they have made have taken them off the path of light and have taken them on the road to the worldly merchants instead. When the time comes to meet the bridegroom, they are on the path to the merchants, not the path to light. Obviously, even when we begin on the path of light, decisions that we make along the way can lead us astray. We must keep vigilant. If we are not in the light at the time of the choice of Heaven, we may be locked out for all time.

The Wedding at Cana

At another wedding feast, Jesus began his ministry and showed his true nature to people beyond the disciples. This first revelation, tellingly, was not in private, not just to people chosen to be followers, but to all the people there.

> There was a wedding in Cana in Galilee, and the mother of Jesus was there. Jesus and his disciples were also invited to the wedding. When the wine ran short, the mother of Jesus said to him, "They have no wine." [And] Jesus said to her, "Woman, how does your concern affect me? My hour has not yet come." His mother said to the servers, "Do whatever he tells you." Now there were six stone water jars there for Jewish ceremonial washings, each holding twenty to thirty gallons.

> Jesus told them, "Fill the jars with water." So they filled them to the brim. Then he told them, "Draw some out now and take it to the headwaiter." So they took it. And when the headwaiter tasted the water that had become wine, without knowing where it came from (although the servers who had drawn the water knew), the headwaiter called the bridegroom and said to him, "Everyone serves good wine first, and then when people have drunk freely, an inferior one; but you have kept the good wine until now." Jesus did this as the beginning of his signs in Cana in Galilee and so revealed his glory, and his disciples began to believe in him. (John 2:1-11)

This is another among the familiar stories of the bible. In the story, wine runs out at the wedding feast and Jesus then turns the water into wine. It is not just a small amount of wine either, it is somewhere between 120 and 180 gallons of wine!

My favorite line in the story, however, is when his mother, Mary, tells the waiters, "Do whatever he tells you." I can imagine a Jewish Mother, or my own Polish Grandmother for that matter, speaking the same way to her children. Mary seemingly ignores the fact that Jesus has just told her that it is not his time to begin his ministry. She completely trusts that Jesus' love for her and for others will move him to provide the assistance that is needed.

Mary speaks to all of us when she says: "Do whatever he tells you." She wants us to follow Jesus all the way to Heaven and she knows that following her son will lead us there.

By seemingly ignoring Jesus' statement that it is not his time yet, Mary shows her complete trust in Jesus' love for her and for all of us. Jesus wants us to have the same confidence in him.

> Jesus tells us: "Whatever you ask in my name, I will do, so that the Father may be glorified in the Son. (John 14:13)

With Jesus to protect us and guide us, we can stand against anything, even things that are harmful or evil.

> Finally, draw your strength from the Lord and from his mighty power. Put on the armor of God so that you may be able to stand firm against the tactics of the devil. (Ephesians 6:10-11)

One final thought on this story. The headwaiter says to Jesus, "Everyone serves good wine first, and then when people have drunk freely, an inferior one; but you have kept the good wine until now." If the headwaiter is correct that the bridegroom has already served the best that he had, then Jesus has given even more on the bridegroom's behalf.

God showers gifts upon us every day of our lives. We should not fear of sharing the best of what we have been given, because no matter how much we share with others, God has greater things in store for us. God will not be outdone in generosity. We can believe that Heaven will be better than anything we will experience here on earth, even better than we can ever imagine.

Parable of the Rich Fool

> Then he [Jesus] told them a parable. "There was a rich man whose land produced a bountiful harvest. He asked himself, 'What shall I do, for I do not have space to store my harvest?' And he said, 'This is what I shall do: I shall tear down my barns and build larger ones. There I shall store all my grain and other goods and I shall say to myself, "Now as for you, you have so many good things stored up for many years, rest, eat, drink, be mer-

> ry!'" But God said to him, 'You fool, this night your life will be demanded of you; and the things you have prepared, to whom will they belong?' Thus will it be for the one who stores up treasure for himself but is not rich in what matters to God." (Luke 12:16-21)

The rich fool is focused only upon how this harvest, that was provided to him from the Lord, will benefit himself. He plans to store up all his riches so that he will live a long, prosperous, and merry life. However, his death precludes his benefit. How much more would he have gained if he had shared his riches? How much more would he have gained if he used his riches to yield a harvest of thirty or sixty or one hundred souls that he cared for on behalf of God?

God will not be outdone in the riches he showers upon all of us. We need to look closely at the riches that God has given to us. Are we focused on the material treasures of this world, or are we "rich in what matters to God?" What matters to God is that we love Him, and we love others. When we focus on what matters to God, we will gladly and willingly give of the gifts we have been given.

> Consider this: whoever sows sparingly will also reap sparingly, and whoever sows bountifully will also reap bountifully. Each must do as already determined, without sadness or compulsion, ***for God loves a cheerful giver***. (2 Corinthians 9:6-7)

God will always save the best for last, so we need not worry about cheerfully giving of the gifts that God has given to us.

The Parable of the Wedding Feast

It is up to us, however, to make decisions in our lives that lead us toward the path of Heaven. None of us is worthy on our own to stand in front of God. It is only through the mercy of God that we may approach him at all. All of us are called to the wedding feast, but not all of us will be ready.

As you read the next story, imagine that the king is God and he is throwing the wedding feast for his son Jesus. The servants who have been dispatched to summon the guests are Moses, or Elijah, other prophets, or even our priests and bishops today.

> Jesus again in reply spoke to them in parables, saying, "The kingdom of heaven may be likened to a king who gave a wedding feast for his son. He dispatched his servants to summon the invited guests to the feast, but they refused to come. A second time he sent other servants, saying, 'Tell those invited: "Behold, I have prepared my banquet, my calves and fattened cattle are killed, and everything is ready; come to the feast."' Some ignored the invitation and went away, one to his farm, another to his business. The rest laid hold of his servants, mistreated them, and killed them. The king was enraged and sent his troops, destroyed those murderers, and burned their city. Then he said to his servants, 'The feast is ready, but those who were invited were not worthy to come. Go out, therefore, into the main roads and invite to the feast whomever you find.' The servants went out into the streets and gathered all they found, bad and good alike, and the hall was filled with guests. But when the king came in to meet the guests he saw a man there not dressed in a wedding garment. He said to him, 'My friend, how is it that you came in here without a wedding garment?' But he was reduced to silence. Then the king said to his attendants, 'Bind his hands and feet, and cast him into the darkness outside, where there will be wailing and grinding

of teeth.' Many are invited, but few are chosen."
(Matthew 22:1-14)

The first thing that comes to mind is, "who are we in the story?" It is easy to quickly dismiss the idea that we would be among the people who refused to come or who would murder the servants. It is easy to assume, of course, that *we* would recognize the invitation for what it is. *We* would go willingly to the wedding feast of Jesus if we were invited by God, wouldn't we?

But, maybe, we are dismissing the invitation, when we dismiss the invitation to go to Mass because of the priest abuse scandal, or because they ask for money, or because of something some priest said or did along the way, or because of any of a thousand other reasons. Are we not willing to "murder" the good servants and ignore God's invitation to the feast of Heaven because of some reason we hold onto so tightly, though it cannot compare to our eternal souls.

Please understand that I am in no way condoning the priest abuse scandal, but I am saying that I am absolutely dedicated to saving *your* eternal soul. That is *the* most important thing ever. I am praying that if such a terrible thing happened to you, that you can find your way back – whatever it takes. However long it takes. Please. Come. Home. There *are* good servants, good priests, who will help you to come back home.

For those of you who have sometimes chosen other things in your life, please reconsider the invitation and join the wedding feast.

For those of you who have not been invited up to this point in your life, for whatever reason, here is your invitation. This is it.

> [The King said:] "'Go out, therefore, into the main roads and invite to the feast whomever you find.' The servants went out into the streets and gathered all they found, bad and good alike, and the hall was filled with guests."

God is looking to fill his feast with guests. He wants *you* to come. He is gathering the "good and the bad alike." Do not be afraid. Please. Come. Home.

But what of the wedding guest that did not come in a wedding garment?

> "But when the king came in to meet the guests he saw a man there not dressed in a wedding garment. He said to him, 'My friend, how is it that you came in here without a wedding garment?' But he was reduced to silence. Then the king said to his attendants, 'Bind his hands and feet, and cast him into the darkness outside, where there will be wailing and grinding of teeth.' Many are invited, but few are chosen."

This, to be fair, is a scary part of the story. What could it possibly mean? The king must have known that when he invited everyone that both bad and good people would be coming, it is only natural. Of course, none of us is worthy to stand in God's presence. We are all human. We are all sinners. God is pure light. We have no ability to stand in the pure light without being destroyed, so how can we do this? Simply, God will help us.

We need to be cleansed first. In our own lives on earth, no one preparing to attend a wedding would do so without first taking a shower or bath and then putting on their best clothes (wedding garment). The man without the wedding garment tries to attend the feast without first cleaning himself and preparing himself.

We are cleansed of our sins by God once we repent and accept God's mercy.

> Jesus said to them in reply, "Those who are healthy do not need a physician, but the sick do. I have not come to call the righteous to repentance but sinners." (Luke 5:31-32)

> Peter [said] to them, "Repent and be baptized, every one of you, in the name of Jesus Christ for the forgiveness of your sins; and you will receive the gift of the holy Spirit. (Acts 2:38)

It is our responsibility to repent and allow God to cleanse us. But, also, it is our responsibility to help others come to be reconciled to God. We are ambassadors for Christ.

> And all this is from God, who has reconciled us to himself through Christ and given us the ministry of reconciliation, namely, God was reconciling the world to himself in Christ, not counting their trespasses against them and entrusting to us the message of reconciliation. So we are ambassadors for Christ, as if God were appealing through us. We implore you on behalf of Christ, be reconciled to God. (2 Corinthians 5:18-20)

On March 23, 2020, I wrote in my journal: "Unworthy to receive God's unconditional love – I felt the power of His love burning so brightly that I dared not draw near – but God wanted me to draw near. When I did, I received the event at Adoration and all the subsequent blessings."

I felt unworthy even to go on the pilgrimage in the first place. I definitely felt unworthy to have received the opportunity to witness the soul on the brink of eternity. I feel unworthy now to write my ideas to you, dear reader. But, at the same time, I feel compelled to share with you what God has shared with me.

The image of the wedding feast applies to going to Mass now, but it also applies to the final feast of Heaven. We must be cleansed before we may enter into Heaven. Our very souls must be washed first in the blood of Jesus before we can put on the robes of Heaven. In the Book of Revelation, which the writer, John, is taken to see Heaven, he tells us:

> Then one of the elders spoke up and said to me, "Who are these wearing white robes, and where did they come from?" I said to him, "My lord, you are the one who knows." He said to me, "These are the ones who have survived the time of great distress; **they have washed their robes and made them white in the blood of the Lamb.**
>
>> "For this reason they stand before
>>   God's throne
>> and worship him day and night in
>>   his temple.
>> The one who sits on the throne will
>>   shelter them."
>
> (Revelation 7:13-15)

This final washing will allow us to stand before God's throne and worship him. To me, this final washing is repentance for our sins in Purgatory. When we meet Jesus at the point of death, and we choose Heaven, very few of us will be worthy to enter Heaven directly. We will immediately understand how unclean we are. We will believe it. We will feel it. We will ache for the harm we have caused to others. We will desire to be cleansed.

Nothing unclean may ever enter Heaven.

> I saw no temple in the city, for its temple is the Lord God almighty and the Lamb. The city had no need of sun or moon to shine on it, for the glory of God gave it light, and its lamp was the Lamb. The nations will walk by its light, and to it the kings of the earth will bring their treasure. During the day its gates will never be shut, and there will be no night there. The treasure and wealth of the nations will be brought there, but nothing unclean will enter it, nor any[one] who does abominable things

or tells lies. Only those will enter whose names are written in the Lamb's book of life. (Revelation 21:22-27)

May you choose Heaven, may you allow yourself to be washed clean by the blood of the lamb.

CHAPTER SIX
Who is Jesus?

Who is Jesus? How do we get to know him? How do we allow Jesus to wash our souls in his blood and make our souls clean?

The beginning of the book of John describes it so well that my words are sorely inadequate. Read this passage slowly and ingest the words.

> ***In the beginning was the Word,***
>   ***and the Word was with God,***
>   ***and the Word was God.***
> He was in the beginning with God.
> All things came to be through him,
>   and without him nothing came to be.
> ***What came to be through him was life,***
>   ***and this life was the light of the human race;***
> ***the light shines in the darkness,***
>   ***and the darkness has not overcome it.***
> A man named John was sent from God. He came for testimony, to testify to the light, so that all might believe through him. He was not the light, but came to testify to the light. The true light, which enlightens everyone, was coming into the world.
> He was in the world,
>   and the world came to be through him,
>   but the world did not know him.
> He came to what was his own,
>   but his own people did not accept him.
> But to those who did accept him he gave power to become children of God, to those who believe in his name, who were born not by natural generation nor by human choice nor by a man's decision but of God.

> *And the Word became flesh*
> *and made his dwelling among us,*
> *and we saw his glory,*
> *the glory as of the Father's only Son,*
> *full of grace and truth.*
>
> John testified to him and cried out, saying, "This was he of whom I said, 'The one who is coming after me ranks ahead of me because he existed before me.'" *From his fullness we have all received, grace in place of grace, because while the law was given through Moses, grace and truth came through Jesus Christ. No one has ever seen God. The only Son, God, who is at the Father's side, has revealed him.* (John 1:1-18)

Jesus is the Word of God made flesh. Jesus has been with us since the beginning of all time and will be with us forever. He is with us because God loves us. He desires that we love him, and each other, and desires that we be together forever.

> *For God so loved the world that he gave his only Son, so that everyone who believes in him might not perish but might have eternal life.* (John 3:16)

I believe with my heart and soul that Jesus is the Son of God. I believe that he is part of the Trinity of the Father, Son and Holy Spirit. I believe that Jesus was sent to save all mankind from our sins, to reconcile each of us with God, and to take each and every one of us to Heaven and give us eternal life. I believe that *it's all true – everything* we have been taught. *Every thing!*

St. Paul describes Christ to us as follows:

> He is the image of the invisible God,
>   the firstborn of all creation.
> For in him were created all things in heaven and on earth,
>   the visible and the invisible,

> whether thrones or dominions or principalities or powers;
>> all things were created through him and for him.
> He is before all things,
>> and in him all things hold together.
> He is the head of the body, the church.
> He is the beginning, the firstborn from the dead,
>> that in all things he himself might be preeminent.
> For in him all the fullness was pleased to dwell,
>> and through him to reconcile all things for him,
>> making peace by the blood of his cross
>> [through him], whether those on earth or those in heaven.
> (Colossians 1:15-20)

That is a lot to take in. Why should you believe me? I am not anybody more important than you. You are just as loved and desired and cherished by God as anyone, as everyone, else. I pray that you ***believe*** that. I pray that you ***feel*** it. I pray that you ***know*** it in your soul and with your entire being.

The Trinity

As a child, one of the first prayers that I learned was to make the Sign of the Cross. As we cross ourselves, we pray:

> ***In the name of the Father, and***
> ***Of the Son, and***
> ***Of the Holy Spirit.***
> ***Amen.***

This prayer is based upon Jesus' commission to the apostles:

> Go, therefore, and make disciples of all nations,
> baptizing them in the name of the Father, and of
> the Son, and of the holy Spirit. (Matthew 28:19)

We begin and end every Mass in this way. We begin our own prayers this way. We are Baptized and receive all the sacraments this way. We have seen sports professionals and others bow their heads and cross themselves this way before beginning a challenging event. We make the Sign of the Cross whenever we think of God and need his help and blessings. We learn that it is a shield of armor against the wickedness that may come to us in this world.

Jesus is one person of the Trinity. One God, three persons. Always united, always distinct.

Although I was taught to believe it, I am not sure that anyone ever really explained to me why I should believe it. How did people come to believe that there was a Trinity of God?

One day, though, praying about the reading of the Conception of Jesus, the message of the Trinity jumped off the page for me. It is the story of the angel Gabriel coming to Mary to announce the birth of Jesus. The words of the story helped me to see what the Gospel writers wanted us to see, what they had come to understand.

The Annunciation

The story is familiar to us. There are so many things to focus on in the story. First, there is an angel of God, and he is sent to a young virgin woman. She is rightly troubled by the sight and by the message that she is to bear a child that will save the Jewish people and rule forever.

> The angel Gabriel was sent from God to a town of Galilee called Nazareth, to a virgin betrothed to a man named Joseph, of the house of David, and the virgin's name was Mary. And coming to her, he said, "Hail, favored one! The Lord is with you." But she was greatly troubled at what was said and pondered what sort of greeting this might be. Then the angel said to her, "Do not be afraid, Mary, for you have found favor with God. Behold, you will

conceive in your womb and bear a son, and you shall name him Jesus. He will be great and will be called Son of the Most High, and the Lord God will give him the throne of David his father, and he will rule over the house of Jacob forever, and of his kingdom there will be no end." But Mary said to the angel, "How can this be, since I have no relations with a man?" And the angel said to her in reply, "*The holy Spirit will come upon you, and the power of the Most High will overshadow you. Therefore the child to be born will be called holy, the Son of God*. And behold, Elizabeth, your relative, has also conceived a son in her old age, and this is the sixth month for her who was called barren; for nothing will be impossible for God." Mary said, "Behold, I am the handmaid of the Lord. May it be done to me according to your word." Then the angel departed from her. (Luke 1:26-38)

There is much for Mary to take in and she asks a question about how this will happen. There, in the angel's answer is the Trinity. I had never seen it before, even though it was right in front of me.

The *holy Spirit* will come upon you, and the power of the *Most High* will overshadow you. Therefore the child to be born will be called holy, *the Son of God*. (Luke 1:35)

The Father is the "Most High." The "holy Spirit" is referenced with "Spirit" capitalized, meaning it is a distinct entity. Finally, Jesus is the child, and he will be called the "Son of God." There is the Trinity, right there in the words. I am certain that biblical scholars have known this for centuries, but to me it was a deeper insight than I had ever seen before. It amazed me. It is one thing to be told that something is true. It is an entirely different thing to discover something to be true for yourself.

At the moment of Jesus' conception, the Father, the Holy Spirit and the Son are all present. At the very moment of Jesus' conception, as God-made-man, all members of the Trinity were part of it.

We can conclude then, that who Jesus was as God, who he was to become as man-God, how he was to die, and how he was to rise were all foretold for centuries by the prophets. The very act of his conception, therefore, was the fulfillment of the prophecies.

Then I went searching for other references to the Trinity in the Bible. There may be more, but I found a few in some very important places.

The Presentation of Jesus in the Temple

When Joseph and Mary take the baby Jesus to the Temple according the Jewish law of Moses, much like a Christian Baptism consecrates a child to the Lord, there is a man there named Simeon who recognizes Jesus as the Messiah. As he cradles Jesus in his arms, he is filled with the Holy Spirit and he praises God that he has seen the Messiah.

> When the days were completed for their purification according to the law of Moses, they took him up to Jerusalem to present him to the Lord, just as it is written in the law of the Lord, "Every male that opens the womb shall be consecrated to the Lord."
>
> Now there was a man in Jerusalem whose name was Simeon. This man was righteous and devout, awaiting the consolation of Israel, and the holy Spirit was upon him. It had been revealed to him by the holy Spirit that he should not see death be-

fore he had seen the Messiah of the Lord. He came in *the Spirit* into the temple; and when the parents brought in the child *Jesus* to perform the custom of the law in regard to him, he took *him* into his arms and blessed *God*, saying:

> "Now, Master, you may let your servant go
>   in peace, according to your word,
> for my eyes have seen your salvation,
>   which you prepared in sight of all
>   the peoples,
> a light for revelation to the Gentiles,
>   and glory for your people Israel."
> (Luke 2:22-23, 25-32)

Luke is very clear: the Holy Spirit, Jesus, and the Father (whom Luke simply refers to as God) are all present at the consecration of Jesus in the Temple.

Another amazing note, Simeon recognizes that the infant Jesus is the "salvation" of all the world, not just the Jews. He sees him as "a light for the revelation to the Gentiles, and glory for your people Israel." While Simeon was a devout Jew, the Holy Spirit reveals to him that Jesus' mission goes well beyond the Jewish people, he is meant to save us all.

The Baptism of Jesus

When Jesus goes to the desert to be baptized by John, we again find the Trinity present in the story.

> After all the people had been baptized and *Jesus* also had been baptized and was praying, heaven was opened and the *holy Spirit* descended upon him in bodily form like a dove. And a *voice came from heaven*, "*You are my beloved Son; with you I am well pleased.*" (Luke 3:21-22)

Again, Jesus, the Holy Spirit, and the Father in heaven are all represented here, are all present in this event.

So too, is not the Trinity present at each baptism. Is not the Trinity present at each of our own baptisms. When a priest, or someone acting in his place in times of emergency, acts in accord with the instruction by Christ to the Apostles, he baptizes us "in the name of the **Father**, and of the **Son**, and of the **holy Spirit**." (Matthew 28:19). To call upon the name of God is to make him present, as when Christ first "said the blessing" before he "broke the bread." (Matthew 26:26)

It is wonderful, is it not, to sit back and just think about the reality of our own baptisms, the presence of God the Father, the Son, and the Holy Spirit. What a blessed thing, for all who have been baptized, the Trinity was there with us, at that moment.

Last Supper Discourses

During the Last Supper before his torture and death, Jesus tells the disciples many things to help them through, not only the next few terrible days, but also into the future. He spends his final time with them summarizing what will happen after he rises to Heaven.

After Jesus washes the feet of the disciples, he tells them that he will send the Holy Spirit to them, just as the Father sent him to them, and that we must accept all three members of the Trinity.

> "From now on I am telling you before it happens, so that when it happens you may believe that *I AM. Amen, amen, I say to you, whoever receives the one I send receives me, and whoever receives me receives the one who sent me.*" (John 13:19-20)

Jesus tells the disciples that the Holy Spirit will be sent, by him, to help them keep God's commandments. When we receive the Holy Spirit, we receive Jesus, we receive the Father. All are one.

"If you love me, you will keep my commandments. And *I will ask the Father*, and he will give you another Advocate to be with you always, the *Spirit of truth*, which the world cannot accept, because it neither sees nor knows it. But you know it, because it remains with you, and will be in you." (John 14:15-17)

"I have told you this while I am with you. *The Advocate, the holy Spirit that the Father will send in my name*—he will teach you everything and remind you of all that [I] told you. Peace I leave with you; my peace I give to you. Not as the world gives do I give it to you. Do not let your hearts be troubled or afraid. You heard me tell you, 'I am going away and I will come back to you.' If you loved me, you would rejoice that I am going to the Father; for the Father is greater than I. And now I have told you this before it happens, so that when it happens you may believe. I will no longer speak much with you, for the ruler of the world is coming. He has no power over me, but the world must know that I love the Father and that I do just as the Father has commanded me." (John 14:25-31)

Dying on the Cross

As Jesus took his very last breaths on the cross, he invokes his Spirit and commends himself and his Spirit to the Father. From the announcement of Jesus' birth through the moment of his death, we find the Trinity.

> Jesus cried out in a loud voice, "*Father,* into your hands *I* commend my *spirit*"; and when he had said this he breathed his last. (Luke 23:46)

In just eight words, Jesus confirms the Trinity of the Father, Son and Holy Spirit.

Jesus, The Good Shepherd

Beyond the Trinity, there are images of the Lord or Jesus as the "Good Shepherd." The very first line of Psalm 23 is, "The Lord is my shepherd," and there are other places as well. A good shepherd guides his sheep, protects them, and cares for them. This image of Jesus as the Good Shepherd can be traced back to Roman times and stays with us still. It is a comforting image.

Quoted in full below is the passage that begins: "I am the good shepherd. A good shepherd lays down his life for the sheep." In this passage, Jesus confirms three things.

First, when he says, "I am the good shepherd," he confirms that he is our Lord over all his flock.

Next, when he says: "A good shepherd lays down his life for the sheep," and "I know mine and mine know me" he confirms that we are his and that he will be here and will protect us always.

Third, he tells us that he was sent to bring all souls into the fold.

Here is the entire passage:

> [Jesus said:] "*I am the good shepherd. A good shepherd lays down his life for the sheep.* A hired man, who is not a shepherd and whose sheep are not his own, sees a wolf coming and leaves the sheep and runs away, and the wolf catches and scatters them. This is because he works for pay and has no concern for the sheep. I am the good shepherd, and I know mine and mine know me, just as the Father knows me and I know the Father; and I will lay down my life for the sheep. I have other sheep that do not belong to this fold. These

> also I must lead, and they will hear my voice, and there will be one flock, one shepherd. This is why the Father loves me, because I lay down my life in order to take it up again. No one takes it from me, but I lay it down on my own. I have power to lay it down, and power to take it up again. This command I have received from my Father." (John 10:11-18)

In nature, sheep learn the voice of their shepherd and follow it, they will not follow the voice of a stranger. Because we belong to Jesus and follow his voice in this world, Jesus will be our shepherd and he will protect us from ruin with his very life.

Depending upon how we lead our lives and where we fall on the continuum from light to darkness, we are more or less likely to recognize Jesus' voice when we have the choice of Heaven or eternal separation from God in Hell. Whose voice will you have trained, during your life, to recognize, and whose voice will be that of the stranger? Will Jesus be your shepherd into the afterlife or will the devil lead your soul into Hell with his empty promises and deceptions?

> "He walks ahead of them, and the sheep follow him, because they recognize his voice. But they will not follow a stranger; they will run away from him, because they do not recognize the voice of strangers." (John 10:4-5)

Also, Jesus tells us that there are others who do not believe in him or seem to follow him in this life but might still be his in the next. We can only imagine that these may include ones who have not heard of Jesus in this life but have followed Him in their hearts. They may be others who have been led away from the church but follow His teachings as they believe them. Since it is not ours to judge God's mercy, there may be many others that we will not understand in this life.

> "I have other sheep that do not belong to this fold.
> These also I must lead, and they will hear my
> voice, and there will be one flock, one shepherd."
> (John 10:16)

The event at Adoration showed me that upon our deaths, everyone will hear the voice of Jesus and be given a chance to follow him to Heaven.

> "My sheep hear my voice; I know them, and they
> follow me." (John 10:27)

God does not want to lose even one soul. Not…Even…One. Jesus tells us:

> "It is not the will of your heavenly Father that one
> of these little ones be lost." (Matthew 18:14)

We are given this ultimate choice. Whether we receive his grace at the moment of death or not, we will still be subject to him at the end of time. This is to fulfill the promise that every knee will bow to the Lord and Savior, Jesus Christ. There will be one shepherd, one flock. At the end of time, even those under the earth, those in Hell, will fully understand that Jesus is Lord.

> God greatly exalted him
>   and bestowed on him the name that is above every name,
>   that at the name of Jesus
> *every* knee should bend,
>   of those in heaven and on earth and under the earth,
>   and *every* tongue confess that
>   Jesus Christ is Lord,
>   to the glory of God the Father.
> (Philippians 2:9-11)

> He is the image of the invisible God,
>   the firstborn of all creation.

> For in him were created all things in heaven and on earth,
>> the visible and the invisible,
>>> whether thrones or dominions or principalities or powers;
>> all things were created through him and for him.
> He is before all things,
>> and in him all things hold together.
> (Colossians 1:15-17)

For since death came through a human being, the resurrection of the dead came also through a human being. For just as in Adam all die, so too in Christ shall all be brought to life, but each one in proper order: Christ the firstfruits; then, at his coming, those who belong to Christ; then comes the end, when he hands over the kingdom to his God and Father, when he has destroyed every sovereignty and every authority and power. For he must reign until he has put all his enemies under his feet. The last enemy to be destroyed is death, for "he subjected everything under his feet." But when it says that everything has been subjected, it is clear that it excludes the one who subjected everything to him. When everything is subjected to him, then the Son himself will [also] be subjected to the one who subjected everything to him, so that God may be all in all. (1 Corinthians 15:21-28)

Doubting Thomas

Many of us have heard the passage that is frequently referred to as "Doubting Thomas." In this story, after the crucifixion of Jesus, the Apostles still did not yet understand the resurrection and had locked themselves away for fear of the Jews. Jesus appears to them in the locked room, but Thomas was not with them at the time.

> Thomas, called Didymus, one of the Twelve, was not with them when Jesus came. So the other disciples said to him, "We have seen the Lord." But he said to them, "Unless I see the mark of the nails in his hands and put my finger into the nail marks and put my hand into his side, I will not believe." Now a week later his disciples were again inside and Thomas was with them. Jesus came, although the doors were locked, and stood in their midst and said, "Peace be with you." Then he said to Thomas, "Put your finger here and see my hands, and bring your hand and put it into my side, and do not be unbelieving, but believe." Thomas answered and said to him, "My Lord and my God!" Jesus said to him, "Have you come to believe because you have seen me? Blessed are those who have not seen and have believed." (John 20:24-29)

Upon our deaths, Jesus will call to all of us, to each of us. He desires that *all* of us believe. He will gently, lovingly say to those who do not yet believe: ***"Put your finger here and see my hands, and bring your hand and put it into my side, and do not be unbelieving, but believe."***

His words are not ridicule, but compassion, yearning. He has compassion and yearning for those who have been led astray and therefore have come to not believe. He has compassion and yearning for those who have never heard the word of God. He has compassion and yearning for those who have led others away from God in their lifetimes. We will all have one more last and lasting chance.

It might be easy to dismiss Thomas as unbelieving, but the story is ***not*** just about the fact that Thomas did not believe. The story is about Jesus being willing to do ***anything*** to help us ***all to*** believe.

Any. Thing. He wants us to put aside any doubts and come with him to Heaven.

> *"Put your finger here and see my hands, and bring your hand and put it into my side, and do not be unbelieving, but believe."* (John 20:27)

There is at least a little bit of Thomas in *all* of us. How sure, how certain, are we that all of this is true? It is beyond wonderful to know that, if we need to see him, and to put our fingers into the nail marks in his hands in order to be sure, Jesus would be willing to grant us that request to help us choose Heaven. What does it mean to us that Jesus would subject himself, not only to the death on the cross, but also to humble himself before us, to wipe away our unbelief, rather than lose our souls to Hell? It means everything. It means love beyond measure.

We can be certain that Jesus is willing to help each of us through any doubts and unbeliefs by looking just a little farther back in the story. The first part of the story describes when Jesus first appeared to the disciples after his death:

> On the evening of that first day of the week, when the doors were locked, where the disciples were, for fear of the Jews, Jesus came and stood in their midst and said to them, "Peace be with you." When he had said this, *he showed them his hands and his side.* The disciples rejoiced when they saw the Lord. (John 20:19-20)

Jesus showed his hands and his side to *all* the disciples who were present. *All* of them. He offers them "peace" and comfort and compassion for their fears and doubts.

When we focus on Thomas' challenge to the reality of the risen Lord, we may miss the point that Jesus showed his wounds to all the disciples to help them believe in everything they had seen and heard. He is willing, as well, to give you the opportunity to examine his wounds, if necessary, for you to make the final choice of Heaven.

This compassion and last chance means that we need to look to Him for our salvation. We cannot walk away. We cannot look away. I pray for the soul at the Adoration event. Though I do not know the outcome of what happened to that soul, I pray that he or she turned back to Jesus and is living life in Heaven. Even in our doubts, Jesus is willing to subject himself to us in order to save us.

For those of us who have followed Jesus as Lord in this lifetime, as the passage reads, we have been "blessed." He tells us, "Blessed are those who have not seen and have believed." With that blessing, there is also an obligation to share that blessing with others. It is our duty on earth to proclaim the good news of Jesus.

> "Go, therefore, and make disciples of all nations, baptizing them in the name of the Father, and of the Son, and of the holy Spirit, teaching them to observe all that I have commanded you. And behold, I am with you always, until the end of the age." (Matthew 28:19-20)

We have received God's choicest blessings, me must, "Therefore," "Go."

Jesus By Many Names

The Christ is called by many names throughout the bible. The names of Jesus give us a glimpse of the power and glory of God in our lives. Sometimes we rush over the names when they are in a passage or a story because we are focused on the story or the message. So here, I have listed a few of his names so that we can take a moment to reflect on the meanings of the Word of God alone.

> Son of God (Matthew 27:54)
>
> Light of the World (John 8:12)

High Priest (Hebrews 6:20)

Capstone (Ephesians 2:20)

Master (Matthew 8:19)

Judge (Acts 10:42)

The Way and the Truth and the Life (John 14:6)

Prince of Peace (Isaiah 9:5)

The Word (John 1:1)

Carpenter (Mark 6:3)

Holy One of God (Mark 1:24)

Emmanuel (Matthew 1:23)

Only Son of God (John 3:18)

Wonder Counselor (Isaiah 9:5)

The Resurrection and the Life (John 11:25)

I AM (John 13:19)

Good Shepherd (John 10:11)

Lamb of God (John 1:29)

The Alpha and the Omega, the First and the Last, the Beginning and the End. (Revelation 22:13)

Advocate (1 John 2:1)

Mediator (1 Timothy 2:5)

Servant (Matthew 12:18)

Bread of Life (John 6:35)

The Amen (Revelation 3:14)

What do these names mean to you in your life? What are other names of Jesus that comfort you? The list could go on, and does go on, as we ponder the love that God has for us and the wonderful gift of his Son.

The Patience of Jesus' Teachings

In John, Chapter 8, we can find several examples of societal contempt of faith and how the scribes and the Pharisees stalk Jesus, try to twist his words, and disavow that he is the Christ. In all these instances, Jesus finds a way to try to move past their unbelief and continue to teach them the truth. As in the Adoration event, Jesus understands the mistakes that the people in the Bible stories are making, and he is trying with all his might to get them to turn around and see that he is the Christ, to see that he can save them.

Jesus is patient with us and our sins. He knows the how and why and what of our sins and understands them, but his focus is not on our punishment, but on our salvation. It is about our forgiveness of self and others, our repentance, and our conversion of mind and soul.

The Woman Caught in Adultery

In the story of the Woman Caught in Adultery, Jesus' patience is clear. He is patient with the sins of the woman, but also how he is so very patient with the sins of the other people in the story.

> Jesus went to the Mount of Olives. But early in the morning he arrived again in the temple area, and all the people started coming to him, and he sat down and taught them. Then the scribes and the Pharisees brought a woman who had been caught in adultery and made her stand in the middle. They said to him, "Teacher, this woman was caught in the very act of committing adultery. Now in the law, Moses commanded us to stone such women.

> So what do you say?" They said this to test him, so that they could have some charge to bring against him. Jesus bent down and began to write on the ground with his finger. But when, they continued asking him, he straightened up and said to them, "Let the one among you who is without sin be the first to throw a stone at her." Again he bent down and wrote on the ground. And in response, they went away one by one, beginning with the elders. So he was left alone with the woman before him. Then Jesus straightened up and said to her, "Woman, where are they? Has no one condemned you?" She replied, "No one, sir." Then Jesus said, "Neither do I condemn you. Go, [and] from now on do not sin any more." (John 8:1-11)

To the accusers and the accused, he acts the same way. He bends down, silent, to leave them to their thoughts. Then, he lifts himself up, and beckons them to lift their thoughts.

Jesus is the "one among" them who is without sin, but he does not "throw a stone at her," he does not condemn her.

Struck by his actions, the crowd chooses to walk away, one by one. As they relent from the evil they were about to do, they choose a path of patience and mercy, just as Jesus is patient and merciful.

Lastly, let us notice that Jesus gives the woman the choice of how she will lead her life going forward. When he says, "Neither do I condemn you. Go, [and] from now on do not sin anymore." He is explaining that it will be her future actions that may condemn her, not him. She has free will, just like the rest of us. It will be our actions that condemn or save us.

Addressing the Jewish Leaders

The next set of passages, though lengthy, demonstrates how patient and truthful Jesus is with the Jewish leaders. When challenged, he does not back down. He does not want to lose their souls. No matter what they say or how they try to twist his words, he calmly explains the truth to them. He is the "light of the world."

> Jesus spoke to them again, saying, ***"I am the light of the world. Whoever follows me will not walk in darkness, but will have the light of life."*** So the Pharisees said to him, "You testify on your own behalf, so your testimony cannot be verified." Jesus answered and said to them, "Even if I do testify on my own behalf, my testimony can be verified, because I know where I came from and where I am going. But you do not know where I come from or where I am going. You judge by appearances, but I do not judge anyone. And even if I should judge, my judgment is valid, because I am not alone, but it is I and the Father who sent me. Even in your law it is written that the testimony of two men can be verified. I testify on my behalf and so does the Father who sent me." So they said to him, "Where is your father?" Jesus answered, "You know neither me nor my Father. If you knew me, you would know my Father also." He spoke these words while teaching in the treasury in the temple area. But no one arrested him, because his hour had not yet come. (John 8:12-20)

How does one explain Heaven to someone else? Jesus has been speaking about the light on the path to eternal life, and the Pharisees challenge him because two people have not corroborated what he has said. They challenge him based upon a law needing two witnesses to an event here on Earth. He replies that he has seen where the Father lives, and the Father has testified to this as well. However closed their minds, Jesus continues to try to reach them.

> Jesus then said to those Jews who believed in him, "If you remain in my word, you will truly be my disciples, and *you will know the truth, and the truth will set you free.*" They answered him, "We are descendants of Abraham and have never been enslaved to anyone. How can you say, 'You will become free'?" Jesus answered them, "Amen, amen, I say to you, everyone who commits sin is a slave of sin. A slave does not remain in a household forever, but a son always remains. So if a son frees you, then you will truly be free. I know that you are descendants of Abraham. But you are trying to kill me, because my word has no room among you. I tell you what I have seen in the Father's presence; then do what you have heard from the Father." (John 8:31-38)

While Jesus is explaining that the "truth will set you free," the people focus on the word "free" and assume he is implying that they are slaves to other humans. They respond by telling him that neither they nor their ancestors have ever been slaves. They cannot comprehend the idea of being a slave to sin, and that by following the truth, they will be freed of the bonds of sin.

> Jesus said to them, "*If God were your Father, you would love me, for I came from God and am here*; I did not come on my own, but he sent me. Why do you not understand what I am saying? Because you cannot bear to hear my word. *You belong to your father the devil and you willingly carry out your father's desires*. He was a murderer from the beginning and does not stand in truth, *because there is no truth in him. When he tells a lie, he speaks in character*, because he is a liar and the father of lies. But because I speak the truth, you do not believe me. Can any of you charge me with sin? If

I am telling the truth, why do you not believe me? ***Whoever belongs to God hears the words of God;*** for this reason you do not listen, because you do not belong to God." (John 8:42-47)

As these passages in John progress, Jesus becomes more clear and more emphatic. In this passage, Jesus tells the crowd that they can choose to either listen to the voice of the Father, through Jesus, or listen to the voice of the devil. People must make a choice.

If we choose to listen to the voice of the devil, we are choosing to believe the lies of a murderer. We must deceive ourselves to believe his lies. That is the character of the devil, that there is "no truth in him."

To follow God, we must be willing to hear and follow the words of truth. These truths can be difficult, but the alternative is lies and an eternal separation from God.

The Eucharist

At the Last Supper with his disciples, Jesus gave us a most wonderful, glorious gift – the gift of himself – in the form of the Eucharist.

Luke first tells us the story of how Jesus and the disciples prepared for the Passover feast. At the end of the story, Jesus gives us his body and blood as a new covenant, a new promise, that through his crucifixion and resurrection he will take us with him to Heaven too.

> When the day of the feast of Unleavened Bread arrived, the day for sacrificing the Passover lamb, he sent out Peter and John, instructing them, "Go and make preparations for us to eat the Passover." They asked him, "Where do you want us to make the preparations?" And he answered them, "When you go into the city, a man will meet you carrying a jar of water. Follow him into the house that

he enters and say to the master of the house, 'The teacher says to you, "Where is the guest room where I may eat the Passover with my disciples?"' He will show you a large upper room that is furnished. Make the preparations there." Then they went off and found everything exactly as he had told them, and there they prepared the Passover.

When the hour came, he took his place at table with the apostles. He said to them, "I have eagerly desired to eat this Passover with you before I suffer, for, I tell you, I shall not eat it [again] until there is fulfillment in the kingdom of God." Then he took a cup, gave thanks, and said, "Take this and share it among yourselves; for I tell you [that] from this time on I shall not drink of the fruit of the vine until the kingdom of God comes." Then he took the bread, said the blessing, broke it, and gave it to them, saying, ***"This is my body, which will be given for you; do this in memory of me." And likewise the cup after they had eaten, saying, "This cup is the new covenant in my blood, which will be shed for you."*** (Luke 22:7-20)

Matthew also shares Jesus' words that, "this is my body," and "this is my blood" of the new covenant with Christ. Jesus' death comes about as a sacrifice for our sins. All of our sins. The new covenant is that Jesus' sacrifice is a promise that all our sins will be forgiven.

While they were eating, Jesus took bread, said the blessing, broke it, and giving it to his disciples said, ***"Take and eat; this is my body."*** Then he took a cup, gave thanks, and gave it to them, saying, ***"Drink from it, all of you, for this is my blood*** of the covenant, which will be shed on behalf of many for the forgiveness of sins." (Matthew 26:26-28)

Catholics believe that at Mass, when the priest blesses the host, or bread, and the wine, they are transformed into the actual body and blood of Christ as at the Last Supper. They are not just symbols of the body and blood, but using the literal words of the Gospels, they are actually the body and blood of Christ.

Therefore, when we receive Communion, we are actually receiving the body, blood, soul and divinity of Jesus into our bodies, just as the disciples did at the Last Supper.

While we will never fully understand the glory of Heaven until we get there, if we have faith in Jesus, and literally believe his words, we will say "yes" to receiving Him. Each time we receive the Eucharist, we say "yes" one more time.

Some Christians believe that the Eucharist is a symbol of the body and blood of Christ. They believe that the bread and wine are not actually transformed into the true body and blood of Jesus at Mass. They struggle, as many have struggled over the centuries, with this glorious mystery. Jesus understood that this would be a difficult idea, so he explained it to them:

> The Jews quarreled among themselves, saying, "How can this man give us [his] flesh to eat?" Jesus said to them, "Amen, amen, I say to you, unless you eat the flesh of the Son of Man and drink his blood, you do not have life within you. Whoever eats my flesh and drinks my blood has eternal life, and I will raise him on the last day. *For my flesh is true food, and my blood is true drink. Whoever eats my flesh and drinks my blood remains in me and I in him.* Just as the living Father sent me and I have life because of the Father, so also

the one who feeds on me will have life because of me. ***This is the bread that came down from heaven.*** Unlike your ancestors who ate and still died, whoever eats this bread will live forever." (John 6:52-58)

At Mass, we all become participants of the new covenant, the new promise of the forgiveness of sins and of the promise of Heaven with Jesus and God. All we need to do to claim that promise is to love our Lord Jesus.

These thoughts take me back to the event at Adoration. The Host grew large in my sight. The monstrance, the golden case that held the host, fell away. The blessed Host *is* Jesus. That was all I saw. It was Jesus, therefore, that grew so large in my sight. It was our Blessed Mother that kept urging me back to her Son.

During those moments at Adoration, I was not actually aware of the people or the music or the church or anything. In a distant, vague kind of way, I knew they were there, but the only reality I knew in that moment was Jesus and the tortured soul. It was as if I was on one side of the curtain and what is normal reality was on the other side.

> To this day, in fact, whenever Moses is read, a veil lies over their hearts, but ***whenever a person turns to the Lord the veil is removed***. Now the Lord is the Spirit, and where the Spirit of the Lord is, there is freedom. All of us, gazing with unveiled face on the glory of the Lord, are being transformed into the same image from glory to glory, as from the Lord who is the Spirit. (2 Corinthians 3:15-4:1)

In my mind's eye, I was speaking directly to Jesus. Pleading with him to save that tortured soul, begging him to save ten souls, a hundred souls, a million souls, a billion souls. A billion souls is still not nearly enough to save all the souls of the earth.

The encounter at St. James was quite overwhelming in physical, mental and spiritual ways. It was physical, through the rosaries in my hands, repeating the prayers, the searing pain in my back and the warm "hug" that told me it was over. It was mental, through "seeing" the Host grow so large in my view and losing all sense of the church and the people around me. It was spiritual, through the encounter with Jesus and the soul, "knowing" that Jesus is there at the moment of death for every soul, and the heartbreak of Jesus as the soul turned away.

I was begging the soul to turn around, to look into Jesus' eyes, to see his love. I felt the agony of Jesus as the soul was turning away. I can still feel the pain of the loss in that moment. It brings tears to my eyes.

Beyond my "begging" – which I believe the tortured soul likely did not hear – I felt powerless to change, or even influence, the outcome. The soul had to choose for himself, it was an act of free will, the ultimate act of free will.

I wonder why the soul was walking away. How did this soul stray so far away from the path toward eternal life that he/she would willingly walk away from Jesus? What could possibly be so compelling, so alluring, in the other direction? It is pure agony to ponder it still.

As I have said before, I have no knowledge of what ultimately happened to that soul. I believe that is not the message we were meant to receive. To me, the message of that moment is that each of us will be given that final choice to choose. At the moment of our death, we will be given one final opportunity to choose between Heaven and Hell. The choice is eternal.

Jesus will be there for us. He will call us. Will we look into Jesus' eyes and accept his embrace? Or, will we be tempted away by evil forces?

For our struggle is not with flesh and blood but with the principalities, with the powers, with the world rulers of this present darkness, with the evil spirits in the heavens. Therefore, put on the armor of God, that you may be able to resist on the evil day and, having done everything, to hold your ground. (Ephesians 6:12-13)

I pray, with all my heart, that you will hold your ground.

We Are All Disciples

One more thought on the Last Supper. One Sunday at Mass, as I was listening to the Eucharistic Prayer, I noticed something in the prayer that I had never really heard with intensity before. I heard the word "disciples." The word "disciples" had always been in the prayer, but my mind had glossed over it.

Part of Eucharistic Prayer II of the Catholic Mass is as follows:

> At the time he was betrayed
> And entered willingly into his Passion,
> He [Jesus] took bread and, giving thanks, broke it,
> And gave it to his *disciples*, saying:
>> Take this, all of you, and eat of it,
>> For this is my Body,
>> Which will be given up for you.
> In a similar way, when supper was ended,
> He took the chalice
> And, once more giving thanks,
> He gave it to his *disciples*, saying:
>> Take this, all of you, and drink from it,
>> For this is the chalice of my Blood,
>> The Blood of the new and eternal covenant,
>> Which will be poured out for you and for many
>> For the forgiveness of sins.
>> Do this in memory of me.

Like many of you, I am sure, the most vivid picture in my head of the Last Supper is based almost entirely on the famous painting by Leonardo da Vinci. In that painting, Jesus is sitting at a table with six apostles on his right and six on his left. It is a long table and they are facing forward, not looking at each other for the most part.

It is not really how people eat dinner with one another unless they are at the head table of a large banquet, but there was little other way for da Vinci to present them all. They are all men, and no one else is in the picture.

So, it seems, I had come to believe on some level, that there was no one else in the room at the Last Supper. While I believed that the Eucharist, the body and blood of Jesus, was meant for all of us, it was quite a leap of faith to jump from the twelve men in that room, to me and you and everyone.

Then one day at Mass, I heard the word "disciples" in the Eucharistic Prayer, not the word "apostles." Disciples is bigger, much bigger. By definition, "disciples" is inclusive of every soul who believes in, and follows, Jesus. By contrast, the term "apostles" was reserved for the twelve closest chosen followers of Jesus.

> He [Jesus] appointed twelve [whom he also named apostles] that they might be with him and he might send them forth to preach. (Mark 3:14)

Of course, we know the twelve apostles were in the room, but they were likely not the only people in the room. In the room were disciples, a larger group. In the words of Luke and Matthew:

> And he [Jesus] answered them, "When you go into the city, a man will meet you carrying a jar of water. Follow him into the house that he enters and say to the master of the house, 'The teacher says to you, "Where is the guest room where I may eat the Passover with my *disciples*?"'" (Luke 22:10-11)

> While they were eating, Jesus took bread, said the blessing, broke it, and **giving it to his disciples** said, "Take and eat; this is my body." Then he took a cup, gave thanks, and gave it to them, saying, "Drink from it, *all of you*, for this is my blood of the covenant, which will be shed **on behalf of many** for the forgiveness of sins. (Matthew 26:26-28)

We do not know from the Gospels how many people were there, but we do know that the Gospels clearly differentiate between the twelve, which are described as the apostles, and the disciples, who were a larger group of followers of Christ.

We can imagine that Jesus' mother and Mary Magdalene were there because they had traveled to Jerusalem with Jesus and they were at the crucifixion the next day. Others would have been there as well because they were followers of Jesus, or were there to serve Jesus and the apostles who were sitting at table.

In these Gospel passages, Jesus gives the Eucharist, not just to the twelve, but to the *disciples*. He says: "Drink from it, *all of you*."

It then occurred to me, I am a disciple of Christ! You are a disciple of Christ! There have been millions, no actually billions, of disciples of Christ throughout the ages, and billions more will come!

Jesus really did give the Eucharist to all of us! When Jesus says: "Drink from it *all of you*." He means *all of us.* We can surmise then, that the Eucharist was given, not just to the apostles, but even to the people who were waiting tables. We can imagine that he gave it not just to the men in the room, but to the women as well!

Those words had been right there, all along, for me to see and hear and believe, but I was blind and deaf to them. The words had become so familiar at Mass that I no longer listened to them. We are all disciples of Christ. We all belong to God, through Jesus. As St. Paul said in his letter to the Galatians:

> For through faith you are all children of God in Christ Jesus. For all of you who were baptized into Christ have clothed yourselves with Christ. There is neither Jew nor Greek, there is neither slave nor free person, there is not male and female; for you are all one in Christ Jesus. (Galatians 3:26-28)

While I have always believed the Eucharist was meant for everyone, reading these words has given me another level of confidence that it is no longer such a leap of faith that the Eucharist is meant for me, you, and all of us. When we participate in the Eucharist, we share in the Last Supper as Jesus commanded us to: "***do this in memory of me.***" (Luke 22:19). No matter who we are, no matter what our circumstances, no matter when we have lived, and no matter where we were born we "***are all one in Christ Jesus.***"

The Resurrection

Jesus would not be our hope, he would not be our Savior, if he had not risen after the crucifixion. Jesus had told the apostles that he would not only be killed by the Jewish leaders, but that he would be raised to life again on the third day.

> He began to teach them that the Son of Man must suffer greatly and be rejected by the elders, the chief priests, and the scribes, and be killed, and rise after three days. (Mark 8:31)

By foretelling, not only his death, but his resurrection, Jesus shows us that he truly has the path to life, the path to Heaven. He truly is the fulfillment of the prophets.

But this was difficult, practically impossible, for the apostles to understand before it happened. It had never happened before, and it has not happened since. It did, however, happen to Jesus, our Savior. How do we know it happened? The Gospels tell us so.

First, to believe that Jesus has risen from the dead, we first need to know and believe Jesus died at the crucifixion and he was buried.

> When it was evening, there came a rich man from Arimathea named Joseph, who was himself a disciple of Jesus. He went to Pilate and asked for the body of Jesus; then Pilate ordered it to be handed over. Taking the body, Joseph wrapped it [in] clean linen and laid it in his new tomb that he had hewn in the rock. Then he rolled a huge stone across the entrance to the tomb and departed. But Mary Magdalene and the other Mary remained sitting there, facing the tomb. (Matthew 27:57-61)

Not only was Jesus' dead body laid in the tomb, the tomb was sealed and guarded on the orders of Pontius Pilate.

> The next day, the one following the day of preparation, the chief priests and the Pharisees gathered before Pilate and said, "Sir, we remember that this impostor while still alive said, 'After three days I will be raised up.' Give orders, then, that the grave be secured until the third day, lest his disciples come and steal him and say to the people, 'He has been raised from the dead.' This last imposture would be worse than the first." Pilate said to them, "The guard is yours; go secure it as best you can." So they went and secured the tomb by fixing a seal to the stone and setting the guard. (Mark 27:62-66)

Jesus had died on Friday and had been buried. The tomb had been guarded over the weekend. The man who they had come to believe in had just been horrifically murdered before their eyes. The disciples were terrified by all that had happened and did not understand all that was going to happen. They did not, could not, really believe that they would see Jesus again.

Yet, on Sunday morning, a few women were the first to see and to hear that Jesus had been raised from the dead.

> When the sabbath was over, Mary Magdalene, Mary, the mother of James, and Salome bought spices so that they might go and anoint him. Very early when the sun had risen, on the first day of the week, they came to the tomb. They were saying to one another, "Who will roll back the stone for us from the entrance to the tomb?" When they looked up, they saw that the stone had been rolled back; it was very large. On entering the tomb they saw a young man sitting on the right side, clothed in a white robe, and they were utterly amazed. He said to them, "Do not be amazed! You seek Jesus of Nazareth, the crucified. He has been raised; he is not here. Behold, the place where they laid him. But go and tell his disciples and Peter, 'He is going before you to Galilee; there you will see him, as he told you.'" (Mark 16:1-7)

The women raced off to tell the apostles what they had seen and heard, but they were still confused.

> So she [Mary of Magdala] ran and went to Simon Peter and to the other disciple whom Jesus loved, and told them, ***"They have taken the Lord from the tomb, and we don't know where they put him."*** (John 20:2)

When Mary of Magdala tells them: "They have taken the Lord from the tomb, and we don't know where they put him," I can just imagine and feel her pain. Her loss was overwhelming. Her grief was unbearable. She was in despair at not knowing what had happened to Jesus.

She truly believed that Jesus was ***Lord***. He was love. He was

Savior. He was Christ. He was Son of the Father. Now, he was simply gone.

Many of us have felt such despair at the loss of a loved one. I, too, have grieved for the loss of loved ones. It is a fully human, agonizing, all-encompassing experience. As humans, we are all subject to these experiences, but when they do come to us, they often come to us as individuals. We can try to be there for one another, but our grief is often felt as our own.

I felt those feelings, too, that night at the Adoration event, the moment I realized that the blessed Host, Jesus, was gone. At the point that Ray was telling me we had to leave, and I discovered that the church was empty, and all the people were gone, I also realized at that moment that the monstrance and the Host were gone as well. It was a moment of agony. They had taken my Lord from the altar, from the church. My very first thought was, "They have taken my Lord away!"

Sometimes, though, we share grief collectively, as the disciples did. We sometimes share these experiences when someone special leaves us, especially, in tragedy. At those moments, we come together to grieve. I think of the death of Pope John Paul II when the whole world seemed to come together to mourn. The death of Martin Luther King, Jr., or John F. Kennedy, or Abraham Lincoln. The deaths of Mother Teresa and Princess Diana brought the whole world together as well.

Being together helped the disciples ease the pain. But, in their grieving and turmoil, the disciples still failed to understand, still failed to fully comprehend what they had been told.

> So Peter and the other disciple went out and came to the tomb. They both ran, but the other disciple ran faster than Peter and arrived at the tomb first; he bent down and saw the burial cloths there, but did not go in. When Simon Peter arrived after him,

> he went into the tomb and saw the burial cloths there, and the cloth that had covered his head, not with the burial cloths but rolled up in a separate place. Then the other disciple also went in, the one who had arrived at the tomb first, and he saw and believed. ***For they did not yet understand the scripture*** that he had to rise from the dead. (John 20:3-9)

In God, however, there is hope, there is salvation. It is that very evening that a group of disciples first encounter the risen Lord.

> On the evening of that first day of the week, ***when the doors were locked, where the disciples were, for fear of the Jews, Jesus came and stood in their midst and said to them, "Peace be with you."*** When he had said this, he showed them his hands and his side. The disciples rejoiced when they saw the Lord. [Jesus] said to them again, "Peace be with you. As the Father has sent me, so I send you." And when he had said this, he breathed on them and said to them, "Receive the holy Spirit. Whose sins you forgive are forgiven them, and whose sins you retain are retained." (John 20:19-23)

This is one of my favorite passages of the entire Bible. The disciples had locked themselves away in a room. They were afraid of the Romans and the Jews, and they felt lost because their beloved leader had been taken from them. Yet, Jesus entered and offered them "peace." Peace. Blessed, cleansing, restful, loving peace. It was a peace that meant that Jesus fully understood all their fears and troubles, and that he would be with them and care for them through all of it.

In my mind, I have always believed that Jesus meets people exactly where they are. He comes through locked doors and locked hearts and cares deeply for all God's children. He cares for you. I wish you peace that only the arms of Our Lord can offer.

There are many passages about the Resurrection of Christ in the Acts of the Apostles and other New Testament books, obviously too many to recount here. In 1 Corinthians, St. Paul summarizes the facts and meaning of the Resurrection of Christ.

> Now I am reminding you, brothers, of the gospel I preached to you, which you indeed received and in which you also stand. Through it you are also being saved, if you hold fast to the word I preached to you, unless you believed in vain. For I handed on to you as of first importance what I also received: that Christ died for our sins in accordance with the scriptures; that he was buried; that he was raised on the third day in accordance with the scriptures; that he appeared to Cephas, then to the Twelve. After that, he appeared to more than five hundred brothers at once, most of whom are still living, though some have fallen asleep. After that he appeared to James, then to all the apostles. Last of all, as to one born abnormally, he appeared to me. (1 Corinthians 15:1-8)

St. Paul continues by telling us that the fact of Jesus' resurrection is the basis of our hope in salvation. He explains that if Jesus had not risen from the dead, that our hope is in vain, and we are still in our sins.

> But if Christ is preached as raised from the dead, how can some among you say there is no resurrection of the dead? If there is no resurrection of the dead, then neither has Christ been raised. And if Christ has not been raised, then empty [too] is our preaching; empty, too, your faith. ***For if the dead are not raised, neither has Christ been raised,***

and if Christ has not been raised, your faith is vain; you are still in your sins. (1 Corinthians 15:12-14, 16-17)

But now Christ has been raised from the dead, the firstfruits of those who have fallen asleep. For since death came through a human being, the resurrection of the dead came also through a human being. For just as in Adam all die, so too in Christ shall all be brought to life, but each one in proper order: Christ the firstfruits; then, at his coming, those who belong to Christ; then comes the end, when he hands over the kingdom to his God and Father, when he has destroyed every sovereignty and every authority and power. For he must reign until he has put all his enemies under his feet. The last enemy to be destroyed is death. (1 Corinthians 15:20-26)

Our faith is not empty. Our belief is not in vain. Jesus **has** risen from the dead. Through our Lord, Christ Jesus, we can rise again to a new life in Heaven.

CHAPTER SEVEN
The Stations of Hope

The many ways that Jesus suffered, both in his life and through the manner of his death, lead us to two important questions. Why was it the will of the Father that Jesus had to be subject to such torture? And, how, then, having suffered so much from us, could Jesus still forgive us, as he did with his words while he was dying on the cross?

> Father, forgive them, they know not what they do. (Luke 23:33)

To understand the answer to the first question of why it was the will of the Father for Jesus to suffer and die for us, we must first come to realize that the manner of his death – all the humiliation, betrayal, torture, and more – represents the worst things that humans can do to one another. It was planned by God and predicted by the prophets. Jesus, though sinless, was sent, in human form, to experience the terrible things that humans can suffer from other humans.

> For our sake he made him to be sin who did not know sin, so that we might become the righteousness of God in him. (2 Corinthians 5:21)

If Jesus could experience those things, accept them, and take them onto himself, he would, in that way, became the sacrificial lamb for all our sins, over all time. This has relevance for our own lives today, if Jesus could forgive the sins he suffered in his life, we can have confidence that he can forgive our sins as well.

This was all foretold by Isaiah some 700 years before Christ:

> ***Yet it was our pain that he bore,***
> ***our sufferings he endured.***

We thought of him as stricken,
   struck down by God and afflicted,
But he was pierced for our sins,
   crushed for our iniquity.
He bore the punishment that makes us whole,
   by his wounds we were healed.
We had all gone astray like sheep,
   all following our own way;
But the LORD laid upon him
   the guilt of us all.
(Isaiah 53:4-6)

David's words in Psalm 22 seem as if he were present at the crucifixion, even though they were written 1,000 years before Christ. The Psalm foretells, not only the crucifixion, but the resulting glory to God and the raising of the dead.

My God, my God, why have you abandoned me?
   Why so far from my call for help,
     from my cries of anguish?
My God, I call by day, but you do not answer;
   by night, but I have no relief.
Yet you are enthroned as the Holy One;
   you are the glory of Israel.
But I am a worm, not a man,
   scorned by men, despised by the people.
All who see me mock me;
   they curl their lips and jeer;
   they shake their heads at me:
"He relied on the LORD—let him deliver him;
   if he loves him, let him rescue him."

Dogs surround me;
   a pack of evildoers closes in on me.
They have pierced my hands and my feet
   I can count all my bones.
They stare at me and gloat;

> *they divide my garments among them;*
> *for my clothing they cast lots.*
> *But you, LORD, do not stay far off;*
> *my strength, come quickly to help me.*
> (Psalm 22:2-4, 7-9, 17-20)

Jesus' torture and death helps us to understand the brutality and pain we can bring to others through our words and actions. It shows us that Jesus fully understands the earthly trials people endure. His suffering and agony, resulting from our own sins, is a call for our remorse and repentance. It also shows us that no matter what we have done, no matter great our sins, *we can* be forgiven.

> But God has thus brought to fulfillment what he had announced beforehand through the mouth of all the prophets, that his Messiah would suffer. *Repent, therefore, and be converted, that your sins may be wiped away*. (Acts 3:18-19)

> *For Christ also suffered for sins once, the righteous for the sake of the unrighteous, that he might lead you to God.* Put to death in the flesh, he was brought to life in the spirit. (1 Peter 3:18)

Jesus understood the gravity of what he was taking on by becoming our Messiah.

> As Jesus was going up to Jerusalem, he took the twelve [disciples] aside by themselves, and said to them on the way, "Behold, we are going up to Jerusalem, and the Son of Man will be handed over to the chief priests and the scribes, and they will condemn him to death, and hand him over to the Gentiles to be mocked and scourged and crucified, and he will be raised on the third day." (Matthew 20:17-19)

> No one has gone up to heaven except the one who has come down from heaven, the Son of Man. And just as Moses lifted up the serpent in the desert, so must the Son of Man be lifted up, so that everyone who believes in him may have eternal life." (John 3:13-15)

When we feel that we have done something so terrible that God cannot ever forgive us, we must take heart that Jesus suffered some of the most terrible things that can be done to a person, not just physically, but emotionally and spiritually as well. In his Divine Mercy, Jesus is standing ready to forgive everyone. ***Every! One!*** He understands, he lived it, he felt it. He feels it today.

> For we do not have a high priest who is unable to sympathize with our weaknesses, but one who has similarly been tested in every way, yet without sin. (Hebrews 4:15)

> We know that Christ, raised from the dead, dies no more; death no longer has power over him. As to his death, he died to sin once and for all; as to his life, he lives for God. Consequently, you too must think of yourselves as [being] dead to sin and living for God in Christ Jesus. (Romans 6:9-11)

This is the answer to the second question of "how" he can still forgive us. It was, and is, his great love for us. It was his mission.

> For Christ...died at the appointed time for the ungodly. Indeed, only with difficulty does one die for a just person, though perhaps for a good person one might even find courage to die. But God proves his love for us in that while we were still sinners Christ died for us. How much more then, since we are now justified by his blood, will we be saved through him from the wrath. (Romans 5:6-9)

Sadly, the troubles and tortures Jesus experienced are still part of life in our age. The fact remains, that we are all sinners. We still do sin and we still suffer the types of things that were done to and were suffered by Jesus. As we reflect on our sins and repent of our sins, we grow closer to one another, and to God and his kingdom.

When we understand that Jesus died "once for all," we come to realize that he died, not just for the sins of others 2,000 years ago, but for the sins we commit today as well. It follows then, that he feels our sins against others and that adds to the pain he suffered. This understanding can help us to be truly repentant for any harm that we have caused.

This knowledge can also help us make our choices on the path to heaven or hell. When we choose a sinful path against others, we choose to add to Christ's suffering.

While Jesus died for all our sins, it is still up to us, up to our free will choice, to accept that forgiveness comes through repentance and the path we take in life.

> Then he opened their minds to understand the scriptures. And he said to them, "Thus it is written that the Messiah would suffer and rise from the dead on the third day and *that repentance, for the forgiveness of sins, would be preached in his name to all the nations*." (Luke 24:45-47)

Repentance for the forgiveness of sins is a critical element of our eternal salvation. Repentance is first an acknowledgment of something wrong. Secondly, it is a desire to change our ways. While we may commit the sin again, and need to repent again, that is a vastly different attitude than thinking, "I am forgiven, therefore, I can do whatever I want."

> For after I turned away, *I repented*;
>   after I came to myself, I struck my thigh;
> *I was ashamed, even humiliated,*

> because I bore the disgrace of my youth.
> (Jeremiah 31:19)

God's salvation is not given to be tossed aside or devalued. It is up to us to graciously accept this ultimate gift.

> Or do you hold his priceless kindness, forbearance, and patience in low esteem, unaware that the kindness of God would lead you to repentance? (Romans 2:4)

In our lives today, sometimes we are the object of the acts that harm us, and sometimes we are the ones that are guilty of the sins that harm others. In either case, God is always with us. He desires with all his heart that we love one another and become reconciled to Him and to one another. He showed us, through his life and his death and resurrection, that he stands with us through it all, and that he still loves and forgives us. We must reach out to meet him too.

If we are the object of sufferings, we can take heart that Jesus walks along with us in our sufferings, and we can then walk with him to paradise.

> But rejoice to the extent that you share in the sufferings of Christ, so that when his glory is revealed you may also rejoice exultantly. (1 Peter 4:13)

Following, is a reflection on the parallels between what Jesus suffered and the sufferings of life in our time. As written, these parallels are not all inclusive, but are meant to help you reflect on ways in which you may be suffering, and the ways in which you may be causing suffering to others.

As you consider these parallels, remember, Jesus died for **_ALL_** of our sins. He can forgive **_YOU_** too! He can give you the courage to forgive others as well.

Let us choose the better way. Let us turn our lives around and be converted. Let us choose forgiveness. Let us choose Jesus!

In Summary, the Suffering of Jesus and the Sufferings of Today will be discussed as follows:

The Sufferings of Jesus

They Twisted Jesus' Words Against Him................................

They Put Their Own Pursuits Above the Worship of God............

They Were Hypocritical..

They Stalked Jesus..

They Wanted to Use Jesus for Their Own Power and Glory..........

They Accused Jesus of Being with the "Wrong" People..............

They Accused Jesus of Having Sinful Motives........................

The Jewish Leaders Wanted Jesus Killed...............................

A Friend Betrayed Jesus..

They Lied in Order to Have Jesus Condemned.......................

They Washed Their Hands of Responsibility........................

They Plotted to Kill Jesus..

They Tortured Jesus; Flogged Him...................................

They Made Jesus Carry His Cross....................................

They Stripped Jesus...

They Mocked Jesus..

Jesus' Friends Abandoned Him..

Jesus' Friends Denied Him...

They Crucified Jesus..

The Sufferings of Today

.... Words on Social Media are Played Against Others

.... Distractions and "Busyness" of Our Lives

.... Saying One Thing and Doing Another

.... Cyber-trolling, Physical Stalking

.... The Seeking of Power

.... We Judge Others and Are Judged by Others

.... Presuming Evil Motives in Others

.... Wishing Death on Others

.... We Betray and Are Betrayed

.... Saying False Things About Others

.... We Look the Other Way

.... Religious Persecutions, Mass Killings

.... Terrorism, Sex Abuse

.... Sexual Slavery, Human Trafficking

.... Sexting, Pornography

.... Bullying, Cyberbullying

.... Abandonment by Loved Ones

.... Elimination of Religion from Our Lives and Communities

.... Abortion

Further meditation on these issues follows:

They Twisted Jesus's Words Against Him

Jesus knew what it was like to have others twist his words so as to encourage others to despise him.

From the Gospel of Luke:

> They watched him closely and sent agents pretending to be righteous who were to trap him in speech, in order to hand him over to the authority and power of the governor. (Luke 20:20)

Today...

It seems that everyone's life is on the internet these days. Words and images are taken out of context and used against another person in an instant. A moment, or a few indiscreet words, can be put out on the internet for all the world to see, and can follow a person for the rest of their lives.

The intent of the posting may be to make oneself feel bigger, or to ridicule, or simply to amuse, but it may not be pleasant or amusing to the one involved. In the end, hearts are wounded, lives may be ruined.

Let us pray to be more mindful of consequences and to turn away from, rather than toward, creating or viewing such hatred.

They Put Their Own Pursuits Above the Worship of God

Sometimes people pursue their own desires rather than the messages and commands of the Lord. Jesus saw how this hurts themselves and others.

Even in the temple area, people were being abused by the money changers and vendors, who were more focused on everyday or selfish concerns.

> They came to Jerusalem, and on entering the temple area he [Jesus] began to drive out those selling and buying there. He overturned the tables of the money changers and the seats of those who were selling doves. He did not permit anyone to carry anything through the temple area. Then he taught them saying, "Is it not written:
>
> 'My house shall be called a house of
>   prayer for all peoples'?
> But you have made it a den of thieves."
> (Mark 11:15-17)

Today...

Are you in a "rat race?" Does it seem like all you do is work? Another deadline. Another dollar. Another debt because we must have the next new thing.

There is no time for your family. No time for relaxation. No time for you. No time for prayer or the Lord.

So many people today are drowning in the burdens of daily life. It is a distraction of the evil one meant to take us away from the important things in our lives.

This is a true suffering. Jesus understands. He wishes for us to stop and come to Him. By doing so, we can find a path that leads us to Heaven. Jesus tells us:

> "Come to me, all you who labor and are burdened, and I will give you rest. Take my yoke upon you and learn from me, for I am meek and humble of heart; and you will find rest for yourselves. For my yoke is easy, and my burden light." (Matthew 11:28-30)

Let us pray to let Jesus ease our burdens, and to be more mindful of the things of Heaven, rather than the things of earth.

They Were Hypocritical

Jesus saw that Jewish leaders twisted the Law of Moses for their own purposes and then acted against their own preaching.

> Then Jesus spoke to the crowds and to his disciples, saying, "The scribes and the Pharisees have taken their seat on the chair of Moses. Therefore, do and observe all things whatsoever they tell you, but do not follow their example. For they preach but they do not practice. They tie up heavy burdens hard to carry and lay them on people's shoulders, but they will not lift a finger to move them." (Matthew 23:1-4)

Today...

Do as I say, not as I do. We remember that saying from our childhoods, but how much more do we see hypocrisy in our lives today.

Where do we see hypocrisy in our lives? We may see it in our politicians, celebrities, workplaces, church and schools.

Where might we be guilty of such hypocrisy? Do we say one thing to our children, or others, and do something else? Do we even recognize it when it happens?

Let us pray to that we have the insight to see the hypocrisy around us and have the courage that Jesus did to call it out.

They Stalked Jesus

In the days of Jesus, the authorities sent people to follow the actions and words of Jesus and intimidate him to change his ways.

> They sent some Pharisees and Herodians to him to ensnare him in his speech. (Mark 12:13)

Today...

Today, there are other weapons in the stalkers' arsenals. Cyber trolling, smartphone apps, GPS, and miniature cameras allow stalkers to follow their victims without detection.

As these weapons have increased in number, so have the consequences to the victims. Feelings of fear and insecurity are just the beginning. All too often, individuals who stalk others may do actual physical harm to the objects of their attention.

Let us pray for all victims of such abuse, and for the conversion of heart of those pursuing others for illicit purposes.

They Wanted to Use Jesus for Their Own Power and Glory

Jesus knew that the disciples could be as guilty of sin as the rest of us. In the Gospel of Mark, we find this scene:

> Then James and John, the sons of Zebedee, came to him and said to him, "Teacher, we want you to do for us whatever we ask of you." He replied, "What do you wish [me] to do for you?" They answered him, "Grant that in your glory we may sit one at your right and the other at your left." When the ten heard this, they became indignant at James and John. (Mark 10:35-37, 41)

Today...

We all know people who use their position of authority for power and control over others. It can happen at levels large and small. From leaders of nations, to a parent over a child, the lure of position and power can be addictive.

But Jesus explains the true role and meaning of leadership in the Gospel of Mark:

> "Whoever wishes to be great among you will be your servant; whoever wishes to be first among you will be the slave of all. For the Son of Man

did not come to be served but to serve and to give his life as a ransom for many." (Mark 10:43-45)

Let us pray for all our leaders and for ourselves, that we may serve others with justice, and according to God's will.

They Accused Jesus of Spending Time With the "Wrong" People

During the time of Jesus, the Jews did not associate with Gentiles (non-Jews) or with people such as tax collectors and prostitutes because they were judged to be "unclean." Additionally, those afflicted with leprosy were banished and made to live outside of their families and communities.

> While he was at table in his house, many tax collectors and sinners sat with Jesus and his disciples; for there were many who followed him. Some scribes who were Pharisees saw that he was eating with sinners and tax collectors and said to his disciples, "Why does he eat with tax collectors and sinners?" (Mark 2:15-16)

Today...

Each of us is judged to be among the "wrong people" at some point in our lives or another. These "pre-judgments" may be hurtful and harmful, but they in no way diminish the inherent dignity of the person who was created in the image of God.

Who today are the most likely to be quickly judged and easily dismissed by our society? The homeless? The drug addicted? The mentally ill? The imprisoned? Immigrants? The poor?

Jesus saw, heard and felt the fear and longings of these discarded people. He saw them as in most need of his care and love.

Let us pray to understand that all of us are loved by God and made in His image. May we show every individual God's love, through our care and our actions.

They Accused Jesus of Acting with Sinful Motives

St. Mark tells us:

> The scribes who had come from Jerusalem said, "He is possessed by Beelzebul," and "By the prince of demons he drives out demons." (Mark 3:22)

St. John also points out their judgment.

> The Jews again picked up rocks to stone him. Jesus answered them, "I have shown you many good works from my Father. For which of these are you trying to stone me?" The Jews answered him, "We are not stoning you for a good work but for blasphemy. You, a man, are making yourself God." (John 10:31-33)

Today...

How often do we make judgments about people who are doing good for others? They are doing that to get noticed. They are trying to butter up the boss or wife. They are trying to act "holier than thou."

God wants us to be a family united in love, to strive for harmony.

Assuming that others have ulterior motives is, in itself, a thought that comes from the evil one.

> But by the *envy* of the devil, death entered the world, and they who are allied with him experience it. (Wisdom 2:24)

Let us pray to understand that we may have differences of opinion or action and still be acting selflessly. Let us remember that it is not our place to judge the motives of others.

The Jewish Leaders Wanted Jesus Killed

There are many references in the Gospels regarding the desire of the authorities to have Jesus killed, including:

> At that time some Pharisees came to [Jesus] and said, "Go away, leave this area because Herod wants to kill you." (Luke 13:31)

> After this, Jesus moved about within Galilee; but he did not wish to travel in Judea, because the Jews were trying to kill him. (John 7:1)

> Jesus said, "The Son of Man must suffer greatly and be rejected by the elders, the chief priests, and the scribes, and be killed and on the third day be raised." (Luke 9:22)

Today...

How many stories do we hear of people receiving threats of harm or death because of their political, religious, or social views? They are threatened because they take a stand for some view that is perceived to threaten another person, or group's, current situation or power.

We can also think of individuals who were actually assassinated because of their leadership, thoughts, or actions. Abraham Lincoln, Dr. Martin Luther King, Jr., and Robert Kennedy come quickly to mind. We can name any number of Saints that were martyred for their beliefs, such as St. Peter or St. Agnes. Killing these men and women did not stop their ideas.

Let us pray for the courage to stand up for our beliefs even in the face of rage and threats by others. Let us also pray for the conversion of heart of those persecuting others for their beliefs.

A Friend Betrayed Jesus

Judas was one of Jesus' closest friends. He had been with him through his ministry and knew his message of the love of God. Yet, he is the one who turned Jesus over to the people he knew wanted to kill him.

As St. Matthew tells us:

> Then one of the Twelve, who was called Judas Iscariot, went to the chief priests and said, "What are you willing to give me if I hand him over to you?" They paid him thirty pieces of silver, and from that time on he looked for an opportunity to hand him over. (Matthew 26:14-16)

Today...

Have you ever felt betrayed by one of your closest friends, or even a brother or sister? How did it feel?

What was the motive of the betrayal? Did they receive approval or reward? Did you receive punishment?

We must keep in mind that the betrayer is never respected by the one who receives the tainted information. Even Judas found he could not return his "blood money" and reverse the evil he had unleashed.

Let us pray for those who have ever betrayed us, and for our own selves when we have committed a similar wrong to others.

They Lied in Order to Have Him Condemned

The Jewish Leaders could not find any true accusations against Jesus, so they resorted to lies.

As St. Mark tells us:

> The chief priests and the entire Sanhedrin kept trying to obtain testimony against Jesus in order to put him to death, but they found none. Many gave false witness against him, but their testimony did not agree. (Mark 14:55-56)

Today...

One of the Ten Commandments is to not bear false witness. You may wonder, among the commandments, is lying on the same level as murder? In many ways it can be.

When someone lies against another it can change his or her entire life. It can ruin his or her reputation in the community. Even worse, if the lie is committed in a court of law, such as was done to Jesus, it can result in incarceration or even death.

Let us pray, that when we feel the urge to gossip, we will stop ourselves. And, if we hear others doing it, we will have the courage to tamp down the flames and urge others to move away from this harmful activity.

They Washed Their Hands of Responsibility

Pontius Pilate was the Roman governor at the time of Jesus. He had all the power of the roman army and government at his command. He believed that Jesus was innocent, and even though he could use force to put down any uprising, he was afraid of the crowd.

Why then, with all that power, would he agree to put a man he found to be innocent to death?

As St. Matthew tells us:

> When Pilate saw that he was not succeeding at all, but that a riot was breaking out instead, he took water and washed his hands in the sight of the crowd, saying, "I am innocent of this man's blood. Look to it yourselves." (Matthew 27:24)

Today...

When do we, or even our leaders, put fear of any kind in front of what we know to be right? When do we neglect to stand up for the innocent when we hear of executions, euthanasia, oppression or other injustices?

How many times have we looked away and washed our hands of responsibility to our fellow man? How many times have we thought such things as: "I personally do not believe in euthanasia, but people have the right to make choices about their own bodies?" Or, "I do not personally believe in the death penalty, but it is the law?"

Before God, we cannot say, "I am innocent of this person's blood." I simply stood by and let them, "look to it" themselves.

Let us pray that we may have the courage to hold ourselves, and our communities, accountable to do what is right, and that we will not let the loud voices of the crowds prevail.

They Plotted to Kill Jesus

After Jesus had raised Lazarus from the dead:

> The chief priests and the Pharisees convened the Sanhedrin and said, "What are we going to do? This man is performing many signs. If we leave him alone, all will believe in him, and the Romans will come and take away both our land and our nation." But one of them, Caiaphas, who was high priest that year, said to them, "You know nothing, nor do you consider that it is better for you that one man should die instead of the people, so that the whole nation may not perish." So from that day on they planned to kill him. (John 11:47-50, 53)

Today...

Since the beginning of time, there have been plots and the actual killing of others for various reasons. Whether it is the persecution of Christians, mass killings in the United States, or murders within families, these tragedies make the news.

It is impossible to fully comprehend the evil that has penetrated these minds and souls that leads to such actions.

Let us pray for all those touched by plots of violence. Let us pray, also, for the souls of those whose minds have been twisted to commit such violence.

They Tortured Jesus; Flogged Him

Pontius Pilate used the tools of the Roman Empire to torture Jesus. As St. John tells us:

> Then Pilate took Jesus and had him scourged. (John 19:1)

A Roman scourging was brutal, bloody, painful, and even life-threatening. Although the Bible gives it but a few words, it is torture that shocks us to our core.

Today...

All too frequently, we hear of terrorist bombings and raids around the world, and even in the United States. The perpetrators may be using bigger, more lethal, weapons, but the message is the same as that of the Romans, "we can, and will kill you, if you do not submit to our way of life."

On a smaller, more individual scale, there is the torture that comes in the form of sexual, mental or physical abuse. These types of torture can come from other members of our families, from coaches, bosses, even priests, or from other individuals we should be able to trust.

What they all have in common is a position of power, and the ability to use power, threats, and fear to get someone to submit to their will.

Let us pray for all those touched by the scourge of terror, and for the conversion of souls for those perpetuating that terror.

They Made Jesus Carry His Cross

What evil must there have been in the minds of men to make someone carry the instrument of his own death? What were they thinking, as well, when they forced a stranger be a party to this evil? As St. John tells us:

> So they took Jesus, and carrying the cross himself he went out to what is called the Place of the Skull, in Hebrew, Golgotha. (John 19:16-17)

St. Matthew expands:

> As they were going out, they met a Cyrenian named Simon; this man they pressed into service to carry his cross. (Matthew 27:32)

Today...

Even today, there is true slavery going on in this world. It is a horrid truth that does not get the attention that it deserves. No one should ever be forced to live as a slave to anyone else.

Whether we are talking about human trafficking, sexual slavery or indentured servitude, these are human beings, not slaves. God understands the plight of these individuals, do we?

Let us pray for those touched by slavery in every form, and that the rest of us open our eyes and put an end to these abuses. Let us also pray for the conversion of the souls of those who are perpetrating these abuses.

They Stripped Jesus

To strip someone is to humiliate them. The authorities wanted Jesus' crucifixion to be as humiliating as possible.

In St. Matthew we find:

> Then the soldiers of the governor took Jesus inside the praetorium and gathered the whole cohort around him. They stripped off his clothes. (Matthew 27:27-28)

Today...

Sexting, pornography, sex in movies, and on television. As a society, we have been laid bare, literally and figuratively, in some grotesque and very hurtful ways.

With smart phones and cameras, it has become very personal for so many. Young people sext pictures of themselves that can land in the hands of sexual predators, or on the internet, for all the world to see.

Our young men are told that viewing pornography is a rite of passage. Our young girls, and women, are dressed in immodest and sexually suggestive ways.

Our young people are told that nudity is normal; it is not. Instead, it leads to humiliation and degradation of spirit.

__Let us pray for a return to the morality and modesty of the human body. Let us pray also for the conversion of heart of those who lure and prey upon the innocent for their own sexual gratification.__

They Mocked Jesus

The Romans and the Jewish leaders mocked Jesus. St. Mark tells us that as Jesus was hanging, brutalized and dying on the cross:

> Those passing by reviled him, shaking their heads and saying, "Aha! You who would destroy the temple and rebuild it in three days, save yourself by coming down from the cross." Likewise the chief priests, with the scribes, mocked him among themselves and said, "He saved others; he cannot save himself. Let the Messiah, the King of Israel, come down now from the cross that we may see and believe." (Mark 15:29-32)

The mockery of Jesus was meant to break his faith and spirit, but it was also meant to be a warning to others who would dare to believe – "this man is a fool and so are you."

Today...

Bullying, cyberbullying, social media, pranks against others – our society sometimes seems awash with people ridiculing others and calling for others to avoid or "cancel" them.

Our young people are often the objects of such mockery, and, unfortunately, may also be the perpetrators of it. The consequences are damaging and long lasting.

We see the frequent mockery of anyone of faith in movies, on talk shows, and even in what passes for news.

What we, and our children, see and hear is that we are meant to bend to the ways of a society that drowns out, or no longer has, faith in God. If we dare to believe in God, we may be considered fools, or that our voices should be silenced.

Let us pray for ourselves and our children to be strong against such bullying. Let us pray, also, that the minds of others will be opened to the Word of God.

Jesus' Friends Abandoned Him

The night before he died, Jesus went to the Garden of Gethsemane with Peter, James and John. There he prayed to God in agony about the persecution he was to about to endure.

Judas came with soldiers to arrest Jesus. As they were taking Jesus away, his friends all left him out of fear.

> And they all left him and fled. (Mark 14:50)

Today...

Divorce, separation, neglect. These are all too common in our world.

Children first learn to trust through the love and commitment of those within their households. Without the constant care of one or more parents, children quickly begin to question their own value.

And, what becomes of these children? They are at far greater risk for poverty, physical and sexual abuse, poor school performance, anxiety, depression, drug use, imprisonment in later life, and even, suicide.

If you have been neglected or abandoned, Jesus understands your pain. He will never leave you; he is with you through it all.

If you have left or abandoned someone, Jesus understands that you likely did it out of your own fears. Trust Jesus to help you turn around and find a path to reconciliation.

Let us pray for Jesus' comfort for all those feeling abandoned, and for those who have left others out of selfishness or fear. Let us pray also for reconciliation and the strengthening of our families.

Jesus' Friends Denied Him

Jesus understands denial. He knew, first hand, what it was like to be denied by someone close to him. He knew it before it even happened. He also knew the pain Peter would experience because of it as well.

On the night of Jesus' trial, Peter remained in the courtyard to be near Jesus, but he was fearful for his own life.

> They lit a fire in the middle of the courtyard and sat around it, and Peter sat down with them. When a maid saw him seated in the light, she looked intently at him and said, "This man too was with him." But he denied it saying, "Woman, I do not know him." A short while later someone else saw him and said, "You too are one of them"; but Peter answered, "My friend, I am not." About an hour later, still another insisted, "Assuredly, this man too was with him, for he also is a Galilean." But Peter said, "My friend, I do not know what you are talking about." Just as he was saying this, the cock crowed, and the Lord turned and looked at Peter; and Peter remembered the word of the Lord, how he had said to him, "Before the cock crows today, you will deny me three times." He went out and began to weep bitterly. (Luke 22:55-62).

Today...

Jesus is that person who loves us the most, more than we can ever imagine. In his heart, we are very close to him. But, when have we denied him too?

The right to acknowledge God is systemically being taken out of our schools, communities, government, workplaces, and even, our speech.

Do we object? Do we remain silent? In what ways do our words, actions, or silence deny Jesus too?

In what ways can we ensure that our children and grandchildren learn the truth of the Gospel?

Jesus will always let us return to him, no matter what we have done or failed to do. We only need turn to him in our weakness, and say we love him.

Let us pray that we will have the courage to acknowledge our Lord and our faith before others. Let us also pray for openness of mind and heart in those who hear the good news.

They Crucified Jesus

As St. Mark tells us:

> Pilate answered, "Do you want me to release to you the king of the Jews?" For he knew that it was out of envy that the chief priests had handed him over. But the chief priests stirred up the crowd to have him release Barabbas for them instead. Pilate again said to them in reply, "Then what [do you want] me to do with [the man you call] the king of the Jews?" They shouted again, "Crucify him." Pilate said to them, "Why? What evil has he done?" They only shouted the louder, "Crucify him." So Pilate, wishing to satisfy the crowd, released Barabbas to them and, after he had Jesus scourged, handed him over to be crucified. (Mark 15:9-15)

Jesus, though innocent, was killed in a most cruel and brutal manner.

Today...

Every day, countless babies, children of God, are aborted in cruel and inhumane ways. The manner of death for these innocents is gruesome to imagine, let alone perform.

As Isaiah prophesied regarding the manner of death of the innocent Jesus, the same may be said of a baby in the womb.

> Though harshly treated, he submitted
>   and did not open his mouth;
> Like a lamb led to slaughter
>   or a sheep silent before shearers,
>   he did not open his mouth.
> Seized and condemned, he was taken away.
>   Who would have thought any more of his destiny?
> For he was cut off from the land of the living,

struck for the sins of his people.
(Isaiah 53:7-8)

We have the power to save the babies or crucify them. In their silence, do they not speak to us?

Let us pray for the souls of all those touched by abortion, especially the babies and their moms and dads. Also, let us pray for the conversion of heart of those who perform, support or fund abortions.

These passages can make us tremendously sad about how the world treated Jesus and how it treats people throughout history and today, but it is also a message of hope. If Jesus can forgive all this, he can forgive us. He can forgive you. He can forgive me.

We must repent our sins and be reconciled to Jesus, our Savior. We must recognize that it is what comes from inside of us that causes sin.

> He summoned the crowd again and said to them, "Hear me, all of you, and understand. Nothing that enters one from outside can defile that person; but the things that come out from within are what defile.
>
> "From within people, from their hearts, come evil thoughts, unchastity, theft, murder, adultery, greed, malice, deceit, licentiousness, envy, blasphemy, arrogance, folly. All these evils come from within and they defile."
>
> (Mark 7:14-16, 21-23)

The sufferings of Jesus throughout his life are meant to be an example to all of us. They are examples of how we can hurt one another, but they also give us clues about the need to turn around, help one another through their trials, and convert to a better way of life and eternity. Jesus understands our hurts because he has lived them himself. He wants to teach us a true way to Heaven.

> I rejoice now, not because you were saddened, but because *you were saddened into repentance*; for you were saddened in a godly way, so that you did not suffer loss in anything because of us. *For godly sorrow produces a salutary repentance without regret,* but worldly sorrow produces death. (2 Corinthians 7:9-10)

I once read a novel in which there was an airplane crash. As the investigators were surveying the scene, one investigator comes upon the body of a woman holding a rosary. He sneers to his colleague, "Well, that really helped her," referring to the rosary. The investigator misses the entire point of the rosary in her hand. The rosary in her hand could not magically save her from the crash, but it may have been of help to her beyond measure. It represents her faith that God will be with her even in her darkest hour, and take her to eternal life.

We cannot hope to fully understand the will of the Father in this lifetime, but we can continue to try. God has given us so much to consider. If possible, in our next life, the trials of our past life may make more sense to us. We think in human terms, God thinks in eternity.

Jesus suffered an earthly death for our sake. However, the love of God, the Father, never left Jesus. He was with Jesus on the cross, in love.

And Jesus has never left us. He is with us in our lives, and trials, and beckons us to follow him. When we do follow him, we will be raised with Jesus to eternal life.

Evil happens. Illness happens. Accidents happen. Natural disasters happen. Wars happen. All the while, our society often has extreme contempt for faith. But evils, disease, death do not ultimately matter. We must continue to believe the truth as spoken in the Bible. No matter what happens, God is there to support us and give us peace. He is there with the promise of eternal life.

Jesus never sneered, or mocked, or ridiculed when he saw human suffering. He touched people, cured people, listened to people, taught people, corrected people, led people, cried with people and raised people up. In other words, he simply loved people. His examples can be ours as we help others who are suffering along the way. None of us will get out of this world without experiencing suffering and even death. Let us be the hands and feet and heart of Jesus here on earth, and help ease each other's suffering along the way.

CHAPTER EIGHT
How Do We Choose Heaven?

There are many steps that we can take along our lifetimes to choose Heaven. God has revealed many of them through the prophets and Jesus has given us even more. Listed here are just a sampling of them.

Do Not Be Afraid. Have No Fear.

God is watching over you. Scholars have found that the message, "do not be afraid," is mentioned, in one form or another, some 365 times in the Bible – once for each day of each year. It is a comforting message that takes us from the first book of the Bible (Genesis) to the very last (Revelation). It is the most consistent message on our pathway to Heaven.

> The word of the LORD came to Abram in a vision: ***Do not fear***, Abram! I am your shield; I will make your reward very great. (Genesis 15:1)

> Then he [God] said: I am God, the God of your father. ***Do not be afraid***. (Genesis 46:3)

> "What I [Jesus] say to you in the darkness, speak in the light; what you hear whispered, proclaim on the housetops. And ***do not be afraid of those who kill the body but cannot kill the soul; rather, be afraid of the one who can destroy both soul and body*** in Gehenna." (Matthew 10:27-28)

> At once [Jesus] spoke to them, "Take courage, it is I; ***do not be afraid***." (Matthew 14:27)

> ***Do not be afraid*** of anything that you are going to suffer. (Revelation 2:10)

God does not want us to let fear of anything in this world lead us away from him. He does, however, want us to keep a watchful eye on Him and his laws so that we stay on the right path. We honor, respect, or "fear," the Lord because he has the power to show us mercy and save our souls from eternal damnation.

> Behold, ***the eye of the LORD is upon those who fear him***,
> upon those who count on his mercy,
> To deliver their soul from death.
> (Psalm 33:18-19)

Jesus' Instruction

In John, Chapter 15, Jesus lays out instructions for the disciples. He explains to them how to remain with him now and forever by following his command to love. He also explains why the world will hate the disciples who follow this guidance. He tells them that it is the work of the Holy Spirit to make the truth known, and that work must be shared by us. This is his path to Heaven.

To Remain in Him

> "*I am the true vine, and my Father is the vinegrower. I am the vine; you are the branches*. Whoever remains in me and I in him will bear much fruit, because without me you can do nothing. Anyone who does not remain in me will be thrown out like a branch and wither; people will gather them and throw them into a fire and they will be burned. If you remain in me and my words remain in you, ask for whatever you want and it will be done for you. By this is my Father glorified, that you bear much fruit and become my disciples." (John 15:1, 5-8)
>
> "*As the Father loves me, so I also love you.* Remain in my love. If you keep my commandments, you will remain in my love, just as I have kept my

Father's commandments and remain in his love.

"I have told you this so that my joy may be in you and your joy may be complete. *This is my commandment: love one another as I love you. No one has greater love than this, to lay down one's life for one's friends.* You are my friends if you do what I command you. I no longer call you slaves, because a slave does not know what his master is doing. I have called you friends, because I have told you everything I have heard from my Father. It was not you who chose me, but I who chose you and appointed you to go and bear fruit that will remain, so that whatever you ask the Father in my name he may give you. This I command you: love one another." (John 15:9-17)

In these passages, Jesus reminds us of both of the two greatest commandments. The first is to love God through loving Jesus. The second is to love each other. When we look to Jesus' teachings, we can see that this message is always there in both his words and his actions. Jesus prays to the Father frequently, and he looks for opportunities to help those around him who are in need. He tells us that we must do the same.

Hatred by the World

"If the world hates you, realize that it hated me first. If you belonged to the world, the world would love its own; but because you do not belong to the world, and I have chosen you out of the world, the world hates you. Remember the word I spoke to you, 'No slave is greater than his master.' If they persecuted me, they will also persecute you. If they kept my word, they will also keep yours. And they will do all these things to you on account of my name, because they do not know the one who

sent me. *If I had not come and spoken to them, they would have no sin; but as it is they have no excuse for their sin.* Whoever hates me also hates my Father. If I had not done works among them that no one else ever did, they would not have sin; but as it is, they have seen and hated both me and my Father. But in order that the word written in their law might be fulfilled, 'They hated me without cause.'" (John 15:18-25)

In this passage, Jesus not only explains that the world will hate us because we follow the teachings of Jesus, but he also gives a warning. He echoes the words of Moses, which are noted earlier in Chapter Four of this book:

See, I have today set before you life and good, death and evil. If you obey the commandments of the LORD... loving the LORD, your God, and walking in his ways... you will live... and the LORD, your God, will bless you....If, however, your heart turns away and you do not obey, but are led astray and bow down to other gods and serve them, I tell you today that you will certainly perish....I have set before you life and death, the blessing and the curse. Choose life, then, that you and your descendants may live. (Deuteronomy 30:15-19)

We have been told of the message and the consequences of not following the teaching. We have been told the truth. If we follow the truth, it will lead us to life everlasting with the Father and Jesus. If, however, we dismiss the truth, we are guilty of great sin and it will lead us on a path of destruction.

The Work of the Holy Spirit

"When the Advocate comes whom I will send you from the Father, *the Spirit of truth* that proceeds

> from the Father, he will testify to me. And *you also testify*, because you have been with me from the beginning." (John 15:26-27)

We need to accept the spirit of truth that has been given to us and that resides in our hearts. We need not only to accept the truth, but to tell it to others as well.

Free Will

From the beginning, God gave everyone free will to choose between life with him and eternal death. He gives us free will in this life to determine the path we will take, and he has clearly laid out the commandments and the new covenant with Jesus as the path to follow toward life. He gives each of us the power to choose.

Jesus reminds us that even he had free will to choose between his service to God and to man. He chose the path that led to his death, but also his resurrection.

> "This is why the Father loves me, because I lay down my life in order to take it up again. No one takes it from me, but *I lay it down on my own. I have power to lay it down, and power to take it up again*. This command I have received from my Father." (John 10:17-18)

Mary, the Mother of Jesus, the most pure among humans, chose to say yes to the Angel Gabriel when he announced that she has been chosen by God to bear the Savior.

> Then the angel said to her, "Do not be afraid, Mary, for you have found favor with God. Behold, you will conceive in your womb and bear a son, and you shall name him Jesus. He will be great and will be called Son of the Most High, and the Lord God will give him the throne of David his father, and he will rule over the house of Jacob forever, and

of his kingdom there will be no end." *Mary said, "Behold, I am the handmaid of the Lord. May it be done to me according to your word."* Then the angel departed from her. (Luke 1:30-32, 38)

We must remember that our path is of our doing and our choice, God will never lead us astray, but he will hold us accountable for our choices.

Do not say: "It was God's doing that I fell away,"
for what he hates he does not do.
Do not say: "He himself has led me astray,"
for he has no need of the wicked.
Abominable wickedness the LORD hates
and he does not let it happen to those who fear him.

God in the beginning created human beings
and made them subject to their own free choice.
If you choose, you can keep the commandments;
loyalty is doing the will of God.
Set before you are fire and water;
to whatever you choose, stretch out your hand.
Before everyone are life and death,
whichever they choose will be given them.

Immense is the wisdom of the LORD;
mighty in power, he sees all things.
The eyes of God behold his works,
and he understands every human deed.
He never commands anyone to sin,
nor shows leniency toward deceivers.
(Sirach 15:11-20)

So submit yourselves to God. Resist the devil, and he will flee from you. (James 4:7)

Be sober and vigilant. Your opponent the devil is prowling around like a roaring lion looking for [someone] to devour. (1 Peter 5:8)

I think about the "golden raindrops" of blessings that are falling all around us. The blessings that I sensed after the Adoration event felt warm like a spring rain, and they were happy to do God's will. They were so pleased to do God's will that when they hit the ground they bounced for joy. These are the blessings that God sends to all of us because he loves each and every one of us so much and he wants us to return to him with all our hearts.

God has given us free will to choose our own paths. We can choose to be just as happy to do the will of God as Jesus, Mary and so many others have, or we can choose a path that leads us away from God. Either way, God will be faithful to us till the end. He continues to shower blessings on the "the righteous and the unrighteous" (Matthew 5:45) in hopes that *all* his children will turn back to him.

How Many Chances?

How many chances will God give us to come back to him? So many chances, we could never count them. When we try and fail, and we turn back to God, and he will welcome us home.

I remember a specific Confession that unburdened my soul and opened my heart to hearing God's messages. At the time of this Confession, I felt that my life was spinning out of control and I was hanging on for dear life. I felt helpless and broken.

I had sought out a priest that was sitting on a short brick wall near a garden. I started the familiar prayers of a Catholic confession. When I got to the part where I was to tell my sins, I told the priest that I felt "broken and wounded inside – that I was seeking God's healing." The priest looked at me directly, with pure love, and no malice, and said, "Being broken is not a sin. Tell me your sins."

> ***Then I declared my sin to you;***
> ***my guilt I covered not.***
> ***I said, 'I confess my faults to the LORD,'***
> ***and you took away the guilt of my sin.***
> (Psalm 32:5)

Then the words of my sins just tumbled out of my mouth. Immediately, the wall in my heart fell, the dam burst. Tears flooded down my cheeks. A heavy weight was lifted off my shoulders. Before those words came out of my mouth, I did not even know that they were in my mind or heart. The door to my heart had been opened the first little crack to experience all there was to find in communion with Jesus Christ!

The priest told me that I had to let go of certain things – to forgive. He said that forgiveness was a choice – a simple choice – as simple as the words in the "Our Father." I felt relieved. Forgiven. Free. Small. Loved. Beloved.

I still felt broken and wounded, but I knew I had opened myself up to letting Jesus help me with these burdens. I did not need to carry them alone!

I thought, I am a sinner. I am a helpless sinner in need of Christ's divine mercy. Forgive me, oh Lord! Thank you for forgiving me! Thank you for forgiving all souls!

But, how many times will our Lord forgive us? How many times must we forgive others? Peter asks Jesus that very question:

> Then Peter approaching asked him, "Lord, if my brother sins against me, how often must I forgive him? As many as seven times?" Jesus answered, "I say to you, not seven times but seventy-seven times." (Matthew 18:21-22)

It is interesting that it is Peter who asks Jesus the questions about the number of times we must forgive because we know specifically that Peter will deny Jesus three times at the crucifixion.

> He said to him, "Lord, I am prepared to go to prison and to die with you." But he replied, ***"I tell you, Peter, before the cock crows this day, you will deny three times that you know me."*** (Luke 22:33-34)

Turn Around and Return to Jesus

Jesus knows all of our sins before we express them. He knows everything. However, when we acknowledge them, we can let them go and turn our lives around.

> [Thus says the Lord:] "I swear I take no pleasure in the death of the wicked, but rather that ***they turn from their ways and live***. Turn, turn from your evil ways! Why should you die?" (Ezekiel 33:11)

Everyone has need to turn around at some points in our lives. Even Peter needed to turn himself around in order to lead the disciples. As Jesus said to Peter:

> "Simon, Simon, behold Satan has demanded to sift all of you like wheat, but I have prayed that your own faith may not fail; and ***once you have turned back, you must strengthen your brothers.***" (Luke 22:31-32)

Jesus wants us all to turn back to him. Like the soul in the Adoration event, we must turn and look into the eyes of Jesus and see His love. It is when we really see his love that we will find our way to the light, to Heaven. But even more, by turning onto the path of light, we can better "strengthen our brothers" and sisters and help lead them to the light.

Jesus knows that even though Peter will sin, he will indeed "turn back" and strengthen all the other disciples after the crucifixion, so he builds his Church around Peter.

> When Jesus went into the region of Caesarea Philippi he asked his disciples, "Who do people say that the Son of Man is?" They replied, "Some say John the Baptist, others Elijah, still others Jeremiah or one of the prophets." He said to them, "But who do you say that I am?" ***Simon Peter said***

> *in reply, "You are the Messiah, the Son of the living God."* Jesus said to him in reply, "Blessed are you, Simon son of Jonah. For flesh and blood has not revealed this to you, but my heavenly Father. *And so I say to you, you are Peter, and upon this rock I will build my church, and the gates of the netherworld shall not prevail against it.*" (Matthew 16:13-18)

Believe in Jesus

The most direct way to eternal salvation is to believe in Jesus Christ and follow his ways. As Peter declares above, Jesus is *the Messiah, the Son of living God*. Belief in Jesus leads us directly to God.

> Jesus cried out and said, "*Whoever believes in me believes not only in me but also in the one who sent me, and whoever sees me sees the one who sent me*. I came into the world as light, so that everyone who believes in me might not remain in darkness. And if anyone hears my words and does not observe them, I do not condemn him, for I did not come to condemn the world but to save the world. *Whoever rejects me and does not accept my words has something to judge him: the word that I spoke*, it will condemn him on the last day, because I did not speak on my own, but the Father who sent me commanded me what to say and speak. And I know that his commandment is eternal life. So what I say, I say as the Father told me." (John 12:44-50)

On the continuum from light to darkness, Jesus is the brightest, purest light of Heaven, the devil is in the darkness. We must continually try to follow the light, be in the light. Every decision we make in our lives leads us toward the light or away from the light. If we reject the light, we condemn ourselves.

By turning toward the light, toward Jesus, we can defeat Satan. However, we should not glory in any way about Satan, we should glory that we are going to Heaven.

> The seventy[-two] returned rejoicing, and said, "Lord, even the demons are subject to us because of your name." Jesus said, "I have observed Satan fall like lightning from the sky. Behold, I have given you the power 'to tread upon serpents' and scorpions and upon the full force of the enemy and nothing will harm you. Nevertheless, do not rejoice because the spirits are subject to you, but rejoice because your names are written in heaven."
>
> At that very moment he rejoiced [in] the holy Spirit and said, "I give you praise, Father, Lord of heaven and earth, for although you have hidden these things from the wise and the learned you have revealed them to the childlike. Yes, Father, such has been your gracious will. All things have been handed over to me by my Father. No one knows who the Son is except the Father, and who the Father is except the Son and anyone to whom the Son wishes to reveal him." (Luke 10:17-22)

But even when we have turned away, God continues to seek us and meet us where we are. Remember, he takes "no pleasure in the death of the wicked, but rather that they turn from their ways and live." (Ezekiel 33:11)

Jesus foretells that Peter would fail in his faith and deny even knowing him three times. He knew other disciples would be "sifted" away by the power of Satan and abandon him during the crucifixion. But, knowing all this, he gives Peter encouragement, and then the directive to turn back and strengthen others. He had chosen Peter to be the leader of the church, the first Pope. He knew that Peter still had much to learn, but he had faith that Peter would return with all his heart.

Here too, in this commissioning of Peter, we can find both the first and second of the greatest commandments. First, turn back, meaning turn your life around and love God with all your heart, soul, mind and body. Second, "strengthen others," use the love of God to love others, help others, take others along with us to Heaven.

Satan will try to "sift" us in his direction, but God is always waiting for us when we turn back. Even when we have taken the wrong path or have even run away, we must believe that we can always return to God. We must have faith in God as he has faith in us. Then we must have faith in each other and love one another.

Receive the Sacraments

Jesus left us special blessings in the form of the Sacraments to hold us fast to him during our lifetimes. These special blessings welcome us into the family of God, bind us to Jesus and his love, and remove our sins so that we may attain the eternal glory of Heaven. According to the time and circumstances of our lives, we should avail ourselves of the Sacraments. By receiving these special blessings, we train ourselves to always recognize the voice of Jesus and remind us to follow the path to Heaven: Baptism, Reconciliation, Eucharist, Confirmation, Holy Orders, Marriage, and Anointing of the Sick.

As we avail ourselves of these special blessings, the closer we will become to God. They help us to remember that we cannot attain Heaven through our own devices, and that we must rely upon God for his care throughout our lives. These blessings also remind us of how we can better serve each other, as brothers and sisters, in the family of God. Lastly, we are reminded that, even when we fail, we can ask for forgiveness and be welcomed with joy back into the good graces of God and our fellow man.

Feed My Sheep

After his resurrection, Jesus appears for the third time to the disciples. During this episode, Jesus takes Peter aside and gives him the chance to atone for his denial of Jesus at the crucifixion. Jesus has long ago forgiven him, as he forgave all of us when he was dying on the cross, but he gives Peter the opportunity to repent and move on to the good works that Jesus has in store for the rest of his life.

> Jesus said to Simon Peter, "Simon, son of John, do you love me more than these?" He said to him, "Yes, Lord, you know that I love you." He said to him, "Feed my lambs." He then said to him a second time, "Simon, son of John, do you love me?" He said to him, "Yes, Lord, you know that I love you." He said to him, "Tend my sheep." He said to him the third time, "Simon, son of John, do you love me?" Peter was distressed that he had said to him a third time, "Do you love me?" and he said to him, "Lord, you know everything; you know that I love you." [Jesus] said to him, "Feed my sheep. (John 21:15-17)

Often in a homily about this passage, much is made of the three times that Jesus asks and the three times Peter responds as being parallel to the three denials of Jesus at his crucifixion. That is clearly part of the story, but, as with any bible passage, there may always be more for us to see.

In this passage, I see the additional message of the two greatest commandments. The first, to love God. The second, to love your neighbor.

Jesus asks: "do you love me?" Because Jesus *is* God as a member of the Trinity, he is asking therefore, "do you love God?" The love of God is the first of the great commandments.

Then he asks him to take care of his flock. That is the second of the great commandments – to love each other. We need to love each other, not just here on earth, but all the way up to Heaven, all the way until we, and they, get to see God face to face. This sums up all that God ever asks.

So, who is included in the flock? It is everyone. It is not only those who know and follow Jesus, but it is also those who need to be brought into the fold.

> My sheep hear my voice; I know them, and they follow me. (John 10:27)

> I have other sheep that do not belong to this fold. These also I must lead, and they will hear my voice, and there will be one flock, one shepherd. (John 10:16)

God tells us that if we love him, we will express our love by tending his sheep, each and every one of them, all the way up to Heaven. It is more than simply a physical tending in which we provide food and shelter, but it is also a spiritual tending of their souls so that they come into the fold of Jesus Christ.

> And all this is from God, who has reconciled us to himself through Christ and given us the ministry of reconciliation, namely, ***God was reconciling the world to himself in Christ, not counting their trespasses against them and entrusting to us the message of reconciliation.*** So we are ambassadors for Christ, as if God were appealing through us. We implore you on behalf of Christ, be reconciled to God. (2 Corinthians 5:18-20)

"Entrusting to us the message of reconciliation." To us. Us. Yes, even today, it is our duty to "be ambassadors of Christ," to proclaim the message of God, of Jesus, of the Holy Spirit.

After Jesus had fed the 5,000, people were following him around. Jesus told them not to follow him because he filled their stomachs, but because he could fill them with eternal life. He wants them to see and do the works of God.

> Jesus answered them and said, "Amen, amen, I say to you, you are looking for me not because you saw signs but because you ate the loaves and were filled. Do not work for food that perishes but for the food that endures for eternal life, which the Son of Man will give you. For on him the Father, God, has set his seal." So they said to him, "What can we do to accomplish the works of God?" Jesus answered and said to them, "This is the work of God, that you believe in the one he sent." (John 6:26-29)

Just so, we need, and want, to do the works of God. If the work of God is to believe in the one he sent, we must believe in Jesus and all his works and all his messages, and we must help others to believe. After Jesus had risen, he appeared to the eleven apostles and told them:

> "Go, therefore, and make disciples of all nations, baptizing them in the name of the Father, and of the Son, and of the holy Spirit, teaching them to observe all that I have commanded you. And behold, I am with you always, until the end of the age." (Matthew 28:19-20)

It is now our job to make disciples of all nations – starting with ourselves and our own families. We need to understand and help others to understand the power of the Father, the Son and the Holy Spirit. We can only do it because Jesus is with us always, until the end of the age.

How to Repent and Receive His Blessings

God spoke to Isaiah and told him to "cry out full-throated and unsparingly" about ways to seek the blessings of God. He wants us to cry out full-throated and let everyone know the path to Him. The desire of God's mercy is expressed in so many ways throughout the Bible.

> ***Cry out full-throated and unsparingly,***
> ***lift up your voice like a trumpet blast.***
>
> ***Then your light shall rise in the darkness,***
> ***and your gloom shall become like midday.***
> (Isaiah 58:1, 10)

> Yet even now— oracle of the LORD—
>   return to me with your whole heart,
>   with fasting, weeping, and mourning.
> Rend your hearts, not your garments,
>   and return to the LORD, your God,
> For he is gracious and merciful,
>   slow to anger, abounding in steadfast love,
>   and relenting in punishment.
> (Joel 2:12-13)

> Have mercy on me, God, in accord with your merciful love;
>   in your abundant compassion blot out my transgressions.
> Thoroughly wash away my guilt;
>   and from my sin cleanse me.
> For I know my transgressions;
>   my sin is always before me.
>
> Against you, you alone have I sinned;
>   I have done what is evil in your eyes…

For you do not desire sacrifice or I would give it;
   a burnt offering you would not accept.
My sacrifice, O God, is a contrite spirit;
   a contrite, humbled heart, O God, you will not scorn.
(Psalm 51:3-6, 18-19)

The Prodigal Son

The story that is sometimes called the "Prodigal Son" is often told at Mass and has many ideas to help us make the choice of Heaven through repentance and forgiveness.

> Then he [Jesus] said, "A man had two sons, and the younger son said to his father, 'Father, give me the share of your estate that should come to me.' So the father divided the property between them. After a few days, the younger son collected all his belongings and set off to a distant country where he squandered his inheritance on a life of dissipation. When he had freely spent everything, a severe famine struck that country, and he found himself in dire need. So he hired himself out to one of the local citizens who sent him to his farm to tend the swine. And he longed to eat his fill of the pods on which the swine fed, but nobody gave him any. Coming to his senses he thought, 'How many of my father's hired workers have more than enough food to eat, but here am I, dying from hunger. I shall get up and go to my father and I shall say to him, "Father, I have sinned against heaven and against you. I no longer deserve to be called your son; treat me as you would treat one of your hired workers."' So he got up and went back to his father. While he was still a long way off, his father caught sight of him, and was filled with compassion. He ran to his son, embraced him and kissed

him. His son said to him, 'Father, I have sinned against heaven and against you; I no longer deserve to be called your son.' But his father ordered his servants, 'Quickly bring the finest robe and put it on him; put a ring on his finger and sandals on his feet. Take the fattened calf and slaughter it. Then let us celebrate with a feast, because this son of mine was dead, and has come to life again; he was lost, and has been found.' Then the celebration began. Now the older son had been out in the field and, on his way back, as he neared the house, he heard the sound of music and dancing. He called one of the servants and asked what this might mean. The servant said to him, 'Your brother has returned and your father has slaughtered the fattened calf because he has him back safe and sound.' He became angry, and when he refused to enter the house, his father came out and pleaded with him. He said to his father in reply, 'Look, all these years I served you and not once did I disobey your orders; yet you never gave me even a young goat to feast on with my friends. But when your son returns who swallowed up your property with prostitutes, for him you slaughter the fattened calf.' He said to him, 'My son, you are here with me always; everything I have is yours. But now we must celebrate and rejoice, because your brother was dead and has come to life again; he was lost and has been found.'" (Luke 15:11-32)

As with many of Jesus' stories there is an interesting and relatable plot. There are great characters: the ungrateful son, the loving father, and the "good" but jealous son. There are also secondary characters: the prostitutes, other citizens, hired workers and the servants.

As you think about the story, also think about where you find yourself in the story.

First, we can glean that the Father in the story is a man of some wealth. He has an estate, property, lands with fields, cattle, servants and hired workers.

With his sons, to whom he has already given their very lives, he shares freely of his wealth. He holds back nothing when the first son asks for "the share of the estate that should come to me," but divides the property between them. However, since we see how much he loves the son, we can imagine the father's agony as the son turns and walks away from him, seemingly happier to have the father's property than his love.

Whatever the temptations that awaited the young man in the distant country, he takes the gifts from the father and "squanders his inheritance on a life of dissipation." A life, let us just say, spent in unsavory behavior.

When the tragedy of the famine strikes the entire country, the young man finally realizes that it had been a gift to be the son of such a generous man, a man who even treats his "hired workers" well.

We all know that part of the story, but what struck me were the son's words to his father. "***Father, I have sinned against heaven and against you.***" To me, he is admitting that he has broken the two greatest commandments, and in effect, we see that he cannot break one without breaking the other. He has harmed his father, his brother, and untold others in the way he has lived his life. And, by harming them, he has demonstrated a disregard for God's love.

Again, we see, the two great commandments are inextricably connected. If we follow one, we follow the other. If we break one, we also break the other.

Next he says, "***I no longer deserve to be called your son; treat me as you would treat one of your hired workers.***" He finally understands that, in the past, he had assumed that what the father gave him was "due" to him, that this was his right; he now understands that all of it had been a gift gladly given. How many times have we assumed, whether consciously or not, that what we have in this life is ours, it is our right, we have worked hard for it? How often have we squandered the gifts that God has given us? How often have we participated in unsavory behavior of one sort or another?

But the son eventually repents. He physically turns around and comes home. The father, upon seeing his son return, is not mad, but instead gives even more. There are gifts for his son and a feast of welcome.

I think about the soul at the Adoration event. He/she had turned away from Jesus, walking away. Was that soul tempted by the evil one to follow some promise of glory or riches or power? Jesus was in agony as the soul was turning away. Jesus desires, beyond measure, to give this soul the gift of eternal life, to give this soul his love.

I have no idea whether that soul turned around toward Jesus. It remains a question unanswered. So, it is for each of us and our souls. At that critical moment when we are choosing between Heaven and Hell, which will we choose? Will we turn back and live?

God has given us the gift of life. He has given us all the gifts in our lives. He does not desire that we are bound to our sins. Can we be like the son in the story and realize our sins before it is too late. If we repent, God will give us everything, including his love, and eternity. We need to turn back to live.

The Workers in the Vineyard

We can get more insight about the good, but jealous, son through the Parable of the Workers in the Vineyard.

"The kingdom of heaven is like a landowner who went out at dawn to hire laborers for his vineyard. After agreeing with them for the usual daily wage, he sent them into his vineyard. Going out about nine o'clock, he saw others standing idle in the marketplace, and he said to them, 'You too go into my vineyard, and I will give you what is just.' So they went off. [And] he went out again around noon, and around three o'clock, and did likewise. Going out about five o'clock, he found others standing around, and said to them, 'Why do you stand here idle all day?' They answered, 'Because no one has hired us.' He said to them, 'You too go into my vineyard.' When it was evening the owner of the vineyard said to his foreman, 'Summon the laborers and give them their pay, beginning with the last and ending with the first.' When those who had started about five o'clock came, each received the usual daily wage. So when the first came, they thought that they would receive more, but each of them also got the usual wage. And on receiving it they grumbled against the landowner, saying, 'These last ones worked only one hour, and you have made them equal to us, who bore the day's burden and the heat.' He said to one of them in reply, 'My friend, I am not cheating you. Did you not agree with me for the usual daily wage? Take what is yours and go. What if I wish to give this last one the same as you? [Or] am I not free to do as I wish with my own money? Are you envious because I am generous?' Thus, the last will be first, and the first will be last." (Matthew 20:1-16)

God's gifts are given freely to all of us. We are all equally unworthy. It is not ours to demand what we receive from God, nor is it ours to judge others as unworthy to receive the gifts they have been given by God.

In the Prodigal Son story, the "good" son resented that the father had given gifts to his brother and then welcomed him home once he had squandered the riches. The good son believed that, because he obeyed his father always, he was more worthy to receive gifts from the father. In the story of the Workers in the Vineyard, the morning laborers, are resentful that they did not receive greater wages than those who have only worked for an hour. Jesus wants us to move beyond these resentments and focus on the bigger picture, our souls. God wants to give all the workers good gifts. God wants to welcome ***all souls*** into Heaven, whether they have believed for a lifetime or for a minute.

In another story:

> Someone in the crowd said to [Jesus], "Teacher, tell my brother to share the inheritance with me." He replied to him, "Friend, who appointed me as your judge and arbitrator?" Then he said to the crowd, "Take care to guard against all greed, for though one may be rich, one's life does not consist of possessions." (Luke 12:13-15)

The greatest "wages" of our time on earth will be our reward of going to Heaven. What these stories are meant to tell us is that we all make choices of how we will live our lives. Even at the moment of death, we can still choose Jesus. We can still choose God. We can still choose Heaven. As Jesus tells us:

> "Do not store up for yourselves treasures on earth, where moth and decay destroy, and thieves break in and steal. But store up treasures in heaven, where neither moth nor decay destroys, nor thieves break in and steal. For where your treasure is, there also will your heart be." (Matthew 6:19-21)

> "No one can serve two masters. He will either hate one and love the other, or be devoted to one and despise the other. You cannot serve God and mammon." (Matthew 6:24)

Remember, we are all laborers of God or the devil. And, at different moments of our lives we may be laborers of one or the other. Sometimes we are on a path consciously, and other times, we may simply be following along. We need to consider how far along the path we have gone. Is it the path we wish to be on?

Our Lord does not ask more of us than we are prepared to give. He tells us, "whoever gives only a cup of cold water to one of these little ones to drink because he is a disciple—amen, I say to you, he will surely not lose his reward." (Matthew 10:42). Jesus is calling you to give just a cup of cold water to quench a thirst. Just a small act of kindness to another may begin the turn to a new path. You know, in your heart, what is right and what is wrong.

As God tells us through the prophet Jeremiah:

> I will **place my law within them, and write it upon their hearts**; I will be their God, and they shall be my people. (Jeremiah 31:33)

Our Lord's law is "written on our hearts," so, if there is **any** good within you, and I am certain there is, then Jesus already knows it, he is always looking for it. It is not too late! If, therefore, you give that "cup of water," that meager act of kindness, your reward can be just as great as that of any saint, because the ultimate reward is Heaven, and it is available to all of us.

Jesus tells us that he has been sent to save **all** souls: "In just the same way, it is not the will of your heavenly Father that one of these little ones be lost." (Matthew 18:14)

Jesus offers each of us, all of us, **you**, the chance to choose Heaven. If you have been working all day in the sun for the kingdom of

God, be glad, be joyous, for the gifts of the Holy Spirit have not been squandered; your reward will be great in Heaven. Do not be jealous of those who have been called later in the day.

If you feel that you try but have only a little to give, do not dismiss the good that you do. Jesus knows your heart. Ask him to help you give all that you can.

If, however, you can see for yourself that you are not using your gifts for good, then now is a "very acceptable time" to make a change, to choose a different path, a path toward your salvation.

> *For he says:*
> *"In an acceptable time I heard you,*
> *and on the day of salvation I helped you."*
>
> *Behold, now is a very acceptable time; behold, now is*
> *the day of salvation.*
> (2 Corinthians 6:2)

Jesus keeps calling you, no matter how late in the day, no matter how late in your life. He will ask you 'Why do you stand here idle all day?' If you answer, 'Because no one has hired us.' He will say "Come."

Can you honestly say that you did not know, that you have not been called, that you do not have gifts to give? Are those the reasons, or have the empty, hollow promises of the evil one led you down the wrong path and left you standing with nothing at the end of the day? Worse yet, are you standing by knowing, in your heart, that "the wages of sin is death." (Romans 6:23)

Our Lord gives you, me, each of us, opportunities every day, every hour to find Him, to choose life, to use your talents for good and to "seek first the kingdom [of God] and his righteousness." (Matthew 6:33)

Jesus will continue to ask, but it is your choice whose voice you will listen to. It is your free will now, and it will be your free will in that final moment. Whose voice has your heart been trained to hear? Jesus is calling even those who have followed the voice of the evil one. He is looking to lead them back to the flock.

> I have other sheep that do not belong to this fold. These also I must lead. (John 10:16)

No matter how far into the darkness you have been led, there, in your heart will always be a shining light. It is Jesus calling you again. Listen for His voice. Follow Him to Heaven.

> My sheep hear my voice; I know them, and they follow me. (John 10:27)

Direct Evidence

There are many, many passages in the Bible that tell us that Jesus has the path to Heaven. A small number are even included in this book. We should not need as many as God has given us, but we are a difficult people to convince. Even so, some of the most direct evidence comes from very direct and reputable sources:

At the Baptism of Jesus, John the Baptist tells us that Jesus will give us the Holy Spirit:

> And this is what he [John] proclaimed: "One mightier than I is coming after me. I am not worthy to stoop and loosen the thongs of his sandals. ***I have baptized you with water; he will baptize you with the holy Spirit.***" (Mark 1:7-8)

Upon Jesus' Baptism, the Father proclaims Jesus to be his Son:

> It happened in those days that Jesus came from Nazareth of Galilee and was baptized in the Jordan by John. On coming up out of the water he saw the heavens being torn open and the Spirit, like a dove, descending upon him. And a voice came from the heavens, ***"You are my beloved Son; with***

you I am well pleased." (Mark 1:9-11)

At the Wedding Feast at Cana, Our Blessed Mother, Mary tells us to: *"Do whatever he tells you."* (John 2:5)

And, Jesus himself tells us: *"I am the way and the truth and the life. No one comes to the Father except through me."* (John 14:6)

Do It Anyway

I will include here a poem on the way to Heaven and the creation of Heaven on earth. This one is from a prayer by Mother Teresa of Calcutta, now a Saint.

You may be familiar with this little poem.

>**<u>Do It Anyway</u>**
>People are often unreasonable and self-centered.
>   *Forgive them anyway.*
>If you are kind, people may accuse you of selfish motives.
>   *Be kind anyway.*
>If you are honest, people may cheat you.
>   *Be honest anyway.*
>If you find happiness, people may be jealous.
>   *Be happy anyway.*
>The good you do today may be forgotten tomorrow.
>   *Do good anyway.*
>Give the world the best you have,
>   and it may never be enough.
>   *Give your best anyway.*
>For you see, in the end, it is between you and God.
>   *It was never between you and them anyway.*

Now, try something different. Replace the person who is the object of the poem with Jesus. As you ponder it, you will see Jesus' life and how he suffered these judgments and jealousies and hostilities while he was on this earth and how he responded.

He still responds to us in the same way today. He shows us by his example that all he did and all he encountered was, and is, to bring our souls closer to Him and to God the Father – anyway.

Jesus Did It Anyway

People were often unreasonable and self-centered.
Jesus forgave them anyway.
When Jesus was kind to the ill or lonely or excluded, people accused him of selfish motives.
Jesus was kind anyway.
When Jesus was honest, people cheated him, even of his life.
Jesus was honest anyway.
When Jesus was happy and proclaimed the glory of God, people were jealous.
Jesus was happy anyway.
The good Jesus did one day was forgotten the next.
Jesus did good anyway.
Jesus gave the world the best he had, and some people are yet to believe.
Jesus gave us his best anyway.
For you see it always was between Jesus and us.
And it will ever be, __for the love of our souls__ – anyway.

…for the love of souls…

　…for the love of souls…

　　…for the love of souls…

Now read the original poem through again slowly, and put yourself into it. It becomes an inspired vision of how we can follow in the footsteps of Jesus through what we encounter in the world and how we can live life always in the presence of God – anyway.

Do It Anyway

People are often unreasonable and self-centered.
Forgive them anyway.

> If you are kind, people may accuse you of selfish motives.
> *Be kind anyway.*
> If you are honest, people may cheat you.
> *Be honest anyway.*
> If you find happiness, people may be jealous.
> *Be happy anyway.*
> The good you do today may be forgotten tomorrow.
> *Do good anyway.*
> Give the world the best you have,
> and it may never be enough.
> *Give your best anyway.*
> For you see, in the end, it is between you and God.
> *It was never between you and them anyway.*

For the Love of Your Soul

The words of St. Paul ring in my ears when I think about what it means to write this book.

> When I came to you, brothers, proclaiming the mystery of God, I did not come with sublimity of words or of wisdom. For I resolved to know nothing while I was with you except Jesus Christ, and him crucified. I came to you in weakness and fear and much trembling, and my message and my proclamation were not with persuasive [words of] wisdom, but with a demonstration of spirit and power, so that your faith might rest not on human wisdom but on the power of God. (1 Corinthians 2:1-5)

I write this for the love of you. I write this for the love of souls – all souls – your soul.

> If I speak in human and angelic tongues but do not have love, I am a resounding gong or a clashing cymbal. And if I have the gift of prophecy and comprehend all mysteries and all knowledge; if I

have all faith so as to move mountains but do not have love, I am nothing. If I give away everything I own, and if I hand my body over so that I may boast but do not have love, I gain nothing. (1 Corinthians 13:1-3)

St. Paul continues this passage with one of the most perfect descriptions of love. If we love others as God loves us, we are surely on the path to Heaven.

> Love is patient, love is kind. It is not jealous, [love] is not pompous, it is not inflated, it is not rude, it does not seek its own interests, it is not quick-tempered, it does not brood over injury, it does not rejoice over wrongdoing but rejoices with the truth. It bears all things, believes all things, hopes all things, endures all things.
>
> Love never fails…
>
> (1 Corinthians 13:4-8)

If you are ever at a loss about what to pray, simply reach out to the Lord and he will meet you wherever you are:

"I do believe, help my unbelief!" (Mark 9:24)

Conclusion

However this writing has come about, I have written it only for the love of you, for the love of all souls. As St. Paul tells us, it is not about *any* thing that I know or write, it is about how God can touch your heart and soul.

The Adoration event has helped me to learn that, *every* thing we need to know about God's love for us has been given to us in the Bible and in the Mass. He speaks to us there. He continually points us there. He tells us the truth. He is there in the true body and blood of Christ in the Eucharist. Seek Him.

> For everyone who asks, receives; and the one who seeks, finds; and to the one who knocks, the door will be opened. (Matthew 7:8 and Luke 11:10)

Maybe some little thing that I have selected and written about here has helped you to get a small glimpse of how much God loves you. Maybe you have your own thoughts and prayers that come from other passages, I pray that you may find them, and they give you and your loved ones comfort.

> If there are prophecies, they will be brought to nothing; if tongues, they will cease; if knowledge, it will be brought to nothing. For we know partially and we prophesy partially, but when the perfect comes, the partial will pass away. When I was a child, I used to talk as a child, think as a child, reason as a child; when I became a man, I put aside childish things. At present we see indistinctly, as in a mirror, but then face to face. At present I know partially; then I shall know fully, as I am fully known. So faith, hope, love remain, these three; but the greatest of these is love. (1 Corinthians 13:8-13)

There will come a time when you are fully known and you are face to face. Then you shall also know fully. May you be ready for it.

This little book is now in the hands of our Father and our Lord Jesus and the Holy Spirit. Where it travels, or even if it travels, is up to Him. I know it has been a journey for me. If it helps one soul, your soul, I will feel humbly, eternally blessed. And, if you have been helped, "Go and do likewise." (Luke 10:37) Amen.

Part III
The Chaplet

CHAPTER NINE
A Chaplet for the Love of Souls

Is it important that we pray? Does anyone listen? Does it help those for whom we pray? Does it help us? Yes, Yes, Yes and Yes.

So, in this time, as in all others, when it is important for us to understand there is a way to choose God and a way to choose against him, to choose between Heaven or Hell, how is it that we should pray? Praying from the heart is of course the best. It is talking to God in the language of love, his language, the language that those who were made in his image were meant to use.

The *Catechism of the Catholic Church* gives us some insight on praying from the heart.

> Where does prayer come from? Whether prayer is expressed in words or gestures, it is the whole man who prays… Scripture speaks… most often of the heart (more than a thousand times). According to scripture, it is the heart that prays. If our heart is far from God, the words of prayer are in vain. (2562)

> The heart is our hidden center, beyond the grasp of our reason and of others; only the Spirit of God can fathom the human heart and know it fully. The heart is a place of decision, deeper than our psychic drives. It is a place of truth, where we choose life or death. (2563)

How can we learn to pray from the heart? What can help us?

> In the same way, the Spirit too comes to the aid of our weakness; for we do not know how to pray as

we ought, but the Spirit itself intercedes with inexpressible groanings. And the one who searches hearts knows what is the intention of the Spirit, because it intercedes for the holy ones according to God's will. (Romans 8:26-27)

Praying to Jesus

With our minds and wills turned toward God, with a desire to pray as we ought, the Spirit within us will help us, even if we cannot express our yearnings well, and Jesus will hear us. It is Jesus who will hear our prayers and it is Jesus who will then intercede for us with his Father.

> Because he [Jesus] remains forever, [he] has a priesthood that does not pass away. ***Therefore, he is always able to save those who approach God through him, since he lives forever to make intercession for them***. (Hebrews 7:24-25)

It is Jesus, then, to whom we would do well to send our prayers. It is Jesus to whom his mother Mary always directs us. It is Jesus to whom Mary directed the children at Fatima when she gave them a prayer directly to her Son.

> *Oh, my Jesus.*
> *Forgive us our sins.*
> *Save us from the fires of Hell.*
> *Lead all souls to Heaven,*
> *Especially those in most need of thy mercy.*
>
> *Amen*

This prayer to Jesus asks him to help lead us to Heaven, to help show us the way, to help us choose Heaven.

It is a prayer that we can easily pray for others, for "those" in need of his mercy. It is also a prayer for our own souls, as we can surely include ourselves among those in need of his mercy. When we pray to Jesus to save loved ones we know well, or for others we do not know at all, we pray to save them from an eternal loss.

This prayer softens our hearts toward those who have wounded us and acknowledges the sins that we have committed that have hurt others. It reminds us that we are all created in the image of God and, even when we do not have the words, we are blessed to have the Holy Spirit lift our inexpressible groanings to the Son, who in turn will take them to the Father.

It is the prayer I said over and over again, rapidly, feverishly at the Adoration event, without being familiar with the prayer and without knowing from where it came. It is this prayer that now forms the heart of what I have come to call the Chaplet for the Love of Souls.

Seeds of the Chaplet

This chaplet was formed during the months following the pilgrimage in 2012, and I believe was a gift directly from Our Blessed Mother. I believe it was her way of helping guide our prayers directly to her son, Jesus.

Our Lady, through apparitions throughout history and throughout the world, wants everyone who has heard her messages to carry her call to prayer to others. On our pilgrimage, at every event, the speaker carried and imparted to us Our Lady's message to pray the Rosary. We were told time and again, that "the Rosary is the most powerful weapon," that the Rosary can stop wars – everywhere - in our families and in the world. While we were on the pilgrimage, we prayed the Rosary every day as a group.

We heard from the priests, that God knows our weaknesses and imperfections, and Our Mother knows her children. Our Father and Our Lady know, that as human beings, we cannot overcome our weaknesses without their love and support. Therefore, our Lord, and his Mother, will help us along the way to become more prayerful. Our prayers need to be for ourselves and others, especially for those who have no one else to pray for them.

One of the priests during the pilgrimage paraphrased the New Testament when he told us, "faith without witness is dead." Our prayers are part of our witness, part of our works.

> So also faith of itself, if it does not have works, is dead. (James 2:17)

I wondered how I could fulfill my part of this mystery. I thought about how this priest talked about both the gifts and the obligations of pilgrimage. He told us that everyone who is called on a pilgrimage is called for a reason. He said, "At some point, you will know the reason, it may be during the trip or afterwards or many years from now." I thought about that night of Adoration at St. James. I knew in my heart and soul that it must be an essential part of the reason for my pilgrimage, but I still did not know where to go with it.

In the weeks and months after we got home from the trip I tried to continue to recite the Rosary on a regular basis, but I struggled. That just baffled me; I could not understand why. I had known how to pray the Rosary since childhood. But, I stumbled every time I tried to say the traditional rosary prayers.

While in the past, I could sometimes feel myself get distracted during a recitation of the Rosary prayers, "distracted" was not the right word for what was happening at that time. My prayers were heartfelt and sincere, they just were not the traditional prayers of the Rosary. I came to believe that these struggles were because our Blessed Mother was trying to teach me something new.

Guidance from Our Lady

Each time I began to say the Rosary, I soon found myself saying the Fatima Prayer on the beads, rather than the Hail Mary, and praying an intention on every bead. This was like the prayers at St. James Church the night of the Eucharistic Adoration. The Fatima Prayer and the intentions were the emerging focus of my prayers.

Our Lady was not trying to tell me that praying the traditional Rosary was wrong. On the contrary, it is arguably the most powerful prayer in the history of mankind and will continue to be so. Our Lady was simply giving us another weapon in our arsenal against evil.

As said the prayers using a set of Rosary beads, it was a process of trial and error. Which prayers are to be used, and in what sequence? Each attempt just did not feel right, and I was confused about where this all was leading. But, I could feel Blessed Mother was with me and she was patient with me. It took until July for me to understand where this was going.

As I prayed, I started to understand my journey at a much deeper level. I started to connect praying the Rosary to three powerful lessons that I had learned, specifically that:

- ***Prayer is the most powerful weapon,***
- ***We need to pray to Jesus directly, and***
- ***We must pray for all souls.***

Over these months, I found myself returning to the Fatima Prayer and praying for specific intentions on each rosary bead. Using the Fatima Prayer seemed so right because of the power and passion that I experienced at Eucharistic Adoration. The prayer she gave the children at Fatima takes our prayers directly to her son, Jesus.

Each time, and every way, that I changed around the order of the prayers, I felt that it was not quite right. I felt, each time, that I was not praying the way that Blessed Mother wanted me to pray. I felt that she was gently urging me, just as she did at Eucharistic Adoration at St. James. I was humbled, and more than a little troubled. What did all this mean?

A Chaplet for All Souls

Then, in the middle of the night on July 27, 2012 I woke up with the Chaplet on my lips, in my heart and in my head. It "sings to the Lord a new song." (cf. Psalm 96) It is a new chaplet, prayed directly to Jesus for ***All Souls***! It is a truly powerful weapon.

That night, around 3:00am, I recorded the Chaplet in my journal and on my computer. It was right, perfect! It was just what Blessed Mother wanted. It was a prayer directly to her Son. It expresses the battle for all souls.

It feels simple. It feels pure. It is a desperate prayer for the desperate and troubled times in our world. It is a prayer for all the souls that are being led astray, and for each of us making everyday decisions that lead us away from the choice for Heaven.

It uses our familiar prayers in a way that feels explosive and powerful. It is a chaplet for the love of souls, the type of love that God feels for them. It is a prayer for ALL souls, because we specifically pray for the troubled souls that have turned against God or are causing pain, not just for the souls receiving the pain.

To pray the Chaplet for the Love of Souls

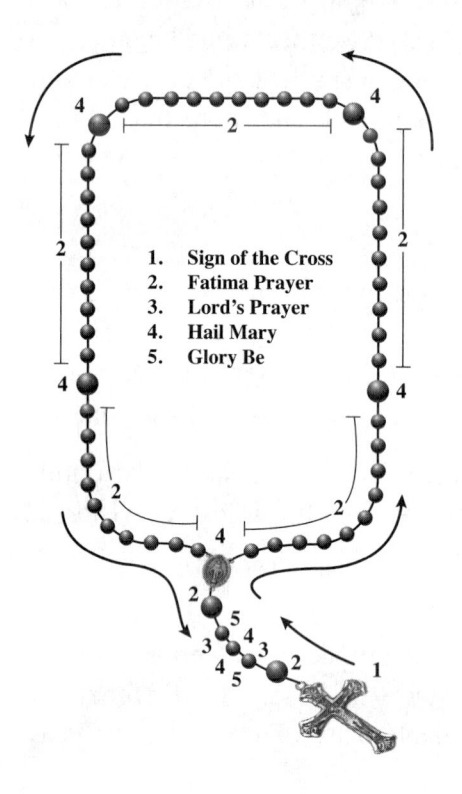

1. Sign of the Cross
2. Fatima Prayer
3. Lord's Prayer
4. Hail Mary
5. Glory Be

In general, pray the **Hail Mary** on the **Our Father** beads of the traditional Rosary, and the **Fatima Prayer** on the traditional **Hail Mary** beads.

On each **Fatima Prayer** bead, mention an intention before the prayer.

When praying in a group, rotate around the group, letting each person mention an intention before the **Fatima Prayer** beads.

There are three quite simple things that make this Chaplet different. (The complete words of the prayers are included in the Appendix for your reference.)

- First, we substitute the Fatima Prayer for the traditional Hail Mary beads on the Rosary; and substitute the Hail Mary for the traditional Lord's Prayer beads. In this way, we pray to Our Lady to help take our prayers to Our Lord, and then make our petitions to Jesus directly.
- Second, before each Fatima Prayer bead, we pray a specific intention. That is 50 intentions! It sounds like a lot, but as you pray the Chaplet you will find that you have so many more. If you pray it in a group of two or more, and you rotate

around the group, you will quickly realize that 50 is not nearly enough! We need to pray for all souls, those who have gone before us, those who are with us now, and those yet to come. The souls before us and after us need our prayers as well as those alive today. It is about saving the world from evil. It is humbling and liberating! It is a truly beautiful and strong and mighty weapon against all the dark forces in the world.

- Lastly, as we pray our intentions, it is important to pray for lost souls, as much as the souls who are in pain. So, for example, if we pray for souls touched by terrorism, we also must pray on the same bead for the people who are perpetrating the terror, that they turn from their current ways and move toward God. I believe now that this is the meaning of the experience at Eucharistic Adoration at St. James – that the soul in the battle could "choose" and that we must pray for those souls to choose God, that they be converted. The only way to have peace in the world is the conversion of the lost.

> "If a man has a hundred sheep and one of them goes astray, will he not leave the ninety-nine in the hills and go in search of the stray? And if he finds it, amen, I say to you, he rejoices more over it than over the ninety-nine that did not stray. In just the same way, it is not the will of your heavenly Father that one of these little ones be lost." (Matthew 18:12-14)

Praying in a Group

> [Jesus told them:] *"For where two or three are gathered together in my name, there am I in the midst of them."* (Matthew 18:20)

Praying the Chaplet in a group multiplies and magnifies the power of our prayers and gives us insight into the trials of those around us. When we join our prayers together and lift them up to the

Lord, we can feel the power of the Holy Spirit within the group, just as Jesus promised us.

In this setting, let each person take a turn praying an intention on the Fatima Prayer beads. Each person may pray a personal intention or a broader intention. There are no right or wrong intentions; there is only what each person feels in his or her heart. That is when we can feel the Chaplet as the most powerful weapon! Then, 50 intentions are not even enough!

Praying the Chaplet Alone

If it helps to get you started, this is how I generally pray the Chaplet when I am alone. My prayers change every time, depending upon the focus of my intentions. Sometimes I just pray one intention, or for the soul in most need of God's mercy.

Remember, there is no right or wrong way. Pray the intentions that are closest to your heart. You may pray for a loved one with cancer, or the return to faith of someone dear to you, or for the forgiveness of your own sins and failings. By just stopping for a moment to reflect on an intention before each prayer bead, it helps to keep your focus and allows you to pray the thoughts weighing on your heart and in the world.

The following is just a frequent way of organizing my thoughts and helping me to be mindful of so many areas in need of prayer and God's healing love.

On the first decade, I often pray for the Church, our priests, our religious, our faith, and for those persecuted for their faith.

> "The harvest is abundant, but the laborers are few; so ask the master of the harvest to send out laborers for his harvest." (Matthew 9:37)

On the second decade, I often pray for leaders around the world, for all their souls. I may pray for specific leaders that they serve

with justice or for nations and peace.

> O God, give your judgment to the king;
>   your justice to the king's son;
> That he may govern your people with justice,
>   your oppressed with right judgment,
> That the mountains may yield their bounty for the people,
>   and the hills great abundance,
> That he may defend the oppressed among the people,
>   save the children of the poor and crush the oppressor.
> (Psalm 72:2-4)

On the third decade, I often pray for souls – especially the souls in most need of God's mercy, for the Holy Souls in Purgatory and for souls who have no one else to pray for them.

Who are the souls in most need of God's mercy? They are all of us. They are the lost, broken, sinful, forgotten. They are our deceased loved ones. They are those doing evil, those fighting evil, those who have turned away from our Lord. They are those in purgatory, those on the brink of Heaven and Hell.

> If you confess with your mouth that Jesus is Lord and believe in your heart that God raised him from the dead, you will be saved.... *"No one who believes in him will be put to shame."...For "everyone who calls upon the name of the Lord will be saved."*

> But how can they call upon him in whom they have not believed? And how can they believe in him of whom they have not heard? And how can they hear without someone to preach? And how can people preach unless they are sent? As it is written, *"How beautiful are [the] feet of those who bring the good news!"* But not everyone has heeded the good news; for Isaiah says, "Lord,

who has believed what was heard from us?" Thus, faith comes from what is heard, and what is heard comes through the word of Christ. But I ask, did they not hear? Certainly they did; for

> *"Their voice goes forth to all the earth, and their words to the ends of the world."*

(Romans 10:9-18)

On the fourth decade, I often pray for all souls touched by evil and for the conversion and redemption of the souls who perpetrate the evil.

In this way, I find I am also praying for the redemption of my own soul, as well as others. I now more fully appreciate that every time I look away and pretend not to see the evil in the world, I am actually perpetuating it.

On the fifth decade, I often pray for individual needs of those I know and love, and for any intentions I have promised to others.

For me, ten just is not enough, so I need to squeeze them together, include them in other decades or start over on the beads!

If I cannot think of anything specific, I simply pray for souls. For the souls in purgatory. For the souls in most need of God's mercy. Sometimes, that is something I just say over and over. As St. James says:

> *"If any one among you should stray from the truth and someone bring him back, he should know that whoever brings back a sinner from the error of his way will save his soul from death and cover a multitude of sins."* (James 5:19-20)

Our prayers to Jesus, if they are in accordance with His will, will be answered.

I am confident that the Lord will bless you, and you will find your own way. Then the blessings will fall around you like warm, golden raindrops that are so happy that they bounce around you.

May God bless you all. Remember,

> ***Behold, now is a very acceptable time; behold, now is the day of salvation.*** (2 Corinthians 6:2)

APPENDIX
Prayers for the Chaplet

The Sign of the Cross

>In the name of the Father, and of the Son, and of the Holy Spirit. Amen.

The Fatima Prayer

Before each Fatima Prayer bead, mention an intention of your heart.

>Oh, my Jesus.
>Forgive us our sins.
>Save us from the fires of Hell.
>Lead all souls to Heaven,
>Especially those in most need of thy mercy.
>Amen.

The Lord's Prayer

>Our Father, who art in Heaven,
>Hallowed be Thy name.
>Thy Kingdom come,
>Thy will be done on earth as it is in Heaven.
>Give us this day our daily bread,
>And forgive us our trespasses,
>As we forgive those who trespass against us.
>And lead us not into temptation,
>But deliver us from evil.
>Amen.

The Hail Mary

>Hail Mary, full of grace, the Lord is with thee.
>Blessed art thou among women, and
>Blessed is the fruit of thy womb, Jesus.

Holy Mary, Mother of God,
Pray for us sinners,
Now and at the hour of our death.
Amen.

The Glory Be

Glory be to the Father, and to the Son,
  and to the Holy Spirit,
As it was in the beginning, is now and ever shall be,
  world without end.
Amen.

To pray the Chaplet for the Love of Souls

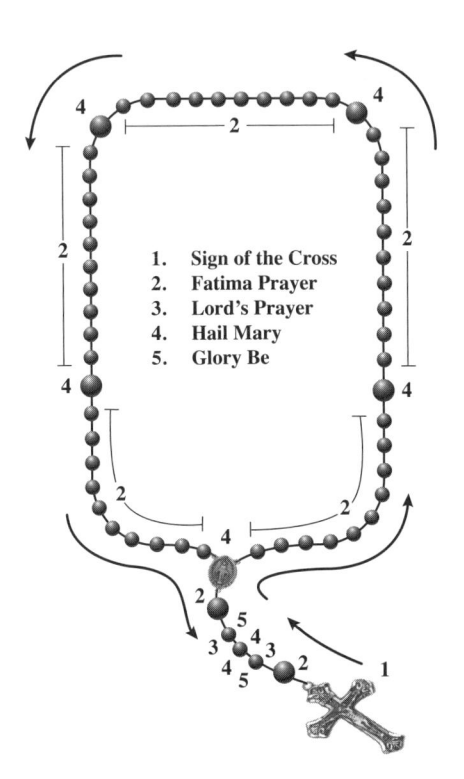

1. Sign of the Cross
2. Fatima Prayer
3. Lord's Prayer
4. Hail Mary
5. Glory Be

In general, pray the **Hail Mary** on the **Our Father** beads of the traditional Rosary, and the **Fatima Prayer** on the traditional **Hail Mary** beads.

On each **Fatima Prayer** bead, mention an intention before the prayer.

When praying in a group, rotate around the group, letting each person mention an intention before the **Fatima Prayer** beads.

Acknowledgments

The author wishes to express her deep gratitude to the untold number of loved ones and friends who have provided their assistance and spiritual support in the preparation of this book, especially:

Cover Art: Original Acrylic Painting by Sister Mary Beth Kemper of the *Sisters of the Most Precious Blood*, O'Fallon, Missouri. 2021. Inspired by a sketch by the author. Prior to publication, a friend pointed out the following passage from the ***Diary of Saint Maria Faustina Kowalska***:

> One day, I saw two roads. One was broad, covered with sand and flowers, full of joy, music and all sorts of pleasures. People walked along it, dancing and enjoying themselves. They reached the end without realizing it. And at the end of the road there was a horrible precipice; that is, the abyss of hell. The souls fell blindly into it; as they walked, so they fell. And their number was so great it was impossible to count them. And I saw the other road, or rather, a path, for it was narrow and strewn with thorns and rocks; and the people who walked along it had tears in their eyes, and all kinds of suffering befell them. Some fell down upon the rocks, but stood up immediately and went on. At the end of the road there was a magnificent garden filled with all sorts of happiness, and all these souls entered there. At the very first instant they forgot all their suffering. (153)

Foreword: Reverend Mitchell Doyen, Pastor, St. John the Baptist Catholic Church, St. Louis, Missouri

Publication: Lu Cortese, Executive Director, and Ann Allen of St. Joseph Evangelization Network, streaming via SJEN.tv and saintjosephradio.net

Author's Photo: Rick Miller, Rick Miller Photography rickmillerphoto.com

Original Music and Production for Stations of Hope: Cathy Pescarino, Assumption of the Blessed Virgin Mary Catholic Church, O'Fallon, Missouri

Spiritual Director: Mickie McCool, Assumption of the Blessed Virgin Mary Catholic Church, O'Fallon, Missouri

Graphics and Formatting: Trese Gloriod, idsign@usa.net

About the Author

Wife. Mother. Grandmother. Diane is a devout Catholic. She has been married to her husband, Ray, for 36 years. They have been blessed with two daughters, Annie and Kathryn. They are also watched over by five babies in Heaven whom they have lovingly named: Alex, Christian, Sam, Angel and Gabriel.

Prior to medical issues which sidelined her career, Diane was an executive overseeing Pay and Benefits for several corporations.

Diane experienced the event at Eucharistic Adoration while on a pilgrimage to a Marian Apparition site in March 2012. She has been writing and speaking on this event and its subsequent blessings ever since. She prays that the story will touch your heart and guide you into a deeper relationship with the Lord.

The author would like to extend a very special thank you to her husband, Ray, for our many years together and for his indispensable assistance in completing this work.

She would also like to thank her family and friends for their love, faith, patience and support throughout this project.

If you have any comments for the author or prayer requests, you may email her at: stationsofhope@gmail.com.

For more information regarding the book or hosting Stations of Hope, please visit Saint Joseph's Evangelization Network at SJEN.tv or saintjosephradio.net.